The Best Damn Pool Instruction Book Period!

by Ron Schneider

Fell

Frederick Fell Publishers, Inc.

2131 Hollywood Boulevard, Suite 305

Hollywood, Florida 33020

954-925-5242

e-mail: fellpub@aol.com

Visit our Web site at www.fellpub.com

This publication is designed to provide accurate and authoritative information in regard to the subject matter covered. It is sold with the understanding that the publisher is not engaged in rendering legal, accounting, or other professional service. If legal advice or other assistance is required, the services of a competent professional person should be sought. From A Declaration of Principles jointly adopted by a Committee of the American Bar Association and a Committee of Publishers.

Library of Congress Cataloging-in-Publication Data

Scneider, Ron, 1944-
  The Best Damn Pool Instruction Book Period!/ by Ron Schneider.
    p. cm.
  ISBN 0-88391-131-0 (trade pbk. : alk. paper)
  1. Gaming. I. General Interest.
  GV995.R55 2004
  796.342--dc22

                    2004010307

The Best Damn Pool Instruction Book Period!

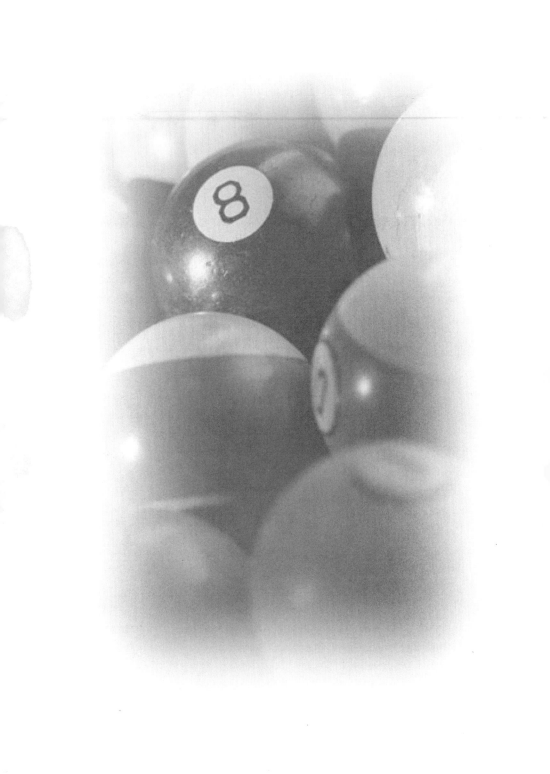

Table of Contents ⸺

Chapter One, The Stroke Builders **1**
This is where it all starts. It is by far the most important chapter in the book.
Without a good solid stroke, you will never excel in your game. Discussion of
the fundamentals of a good stroke and various illustrated practice routines
will help you develop a smooth, accurate, and enviable stroke. Having a
pool table or access to a pool table is a must topractice and develop the
"muscle memory" necessary for a good stroke.

Chapter Two, The Practice Shots **15**
This chapter takes the stroke builders to the next level. Each practice shot
will give you immediate feedback and develop "memory routines" to be
used in game situations. Most of these practice shots come up time and
time again and must be executed well to improve your winning
percentage.

Chapter Three, Safety Play **31**
Safeties are an overlooked and important part of the game. Knowing, and
most importantly practicing these basic safeties is a must when playing any
competitive pool game. Executing a good safety is sometimes better than
making the shot. This is especially true if your opponent does not know the
kicking systems illustrated in Chapter 4.

Chapter Four, The Kicking Game •••••••••••••••••••••••••••••••••••••• **49**
The worst thing you can do in 9 ball is give up "ball-in-hand". This chapter will discuss simple 1, 2, 3, and even 4 rail kicking systems that you don't need a degree in higher math or a calculator to figure out. I call this the "WORLD OF PARALLELS". These simple systems will have you not just trying to kick to hit a hidden ball, but you will now start to even make some of these shots. This is the largest chapter in the book with 50 pages of illustrated diagrams.

Chapter Five, Banking ••**101**
Here I will discuss and illustrate at length why banking is so difficult. But, after learning the "WORLD OF PARALLELS" in Chapter 4, banking now becomes much easier. Now banking simply becomes recognizing the angle and proper stroking of the cue ball.

Chapter Six, Combinations •• **121**
Like banks, combinations are also very difficult. Discussion and illustration of 5 different types of systems will make shooting these a little easier. Do you have a system or how many systems do you know?

Chapter Seven, Caroms ••• **131**
Here the two most important things to know are:
> 1. Actually recognizing the carom shot
> 2. Understanding the "tangent line"

Again there will be discussion and illustration of several types of systems to help improve your pocketing skills.

Chapter Eight, The Nine Ball Break **145**
Generally speaking when the professionals play, the one breaking the best usually wins. Here I will discuss the key points for a good break and also illustrate some legal racking techniques which can give you a slight edge. If your break is weak or if you scratch a lot, this chapter is a must.

Chapter Nine, The Masse Shot **153**
When all your options (jumping, kicking, etc,) are blocked, sometimes you just have to bend the cue ball around another object ball. With a little instruction and practice, you can easily add the masse shot to your arsenal.

Chapter Ten, The Jump Shot **159**
If you are going to really improve your game, you must have a jump shot in your repertoire. With the right equipment and instruction, this area of the game is not as difficult as it looks.

Chapter Eleven, Position Play **169**
When a novice watches a professional run a rack, the normal reaction is to say, "Boy that was an easy rack--he never had a tough shot!" He does not understand how difficult it is to move "whitey" around the table to an exact location. The keys to this chapter are theunderstanding of the tangent line and the english and speed needed on the cue ball. The illustrated drills discussed in this chapter will show you how to gain better control of thecue ball.

Chapter Twelve, Specialty Shots 195

These are not trick shots but shots that you must be able to execute if you are going to play the game at a higher level. These illustrated shots come up more often than you think. Most require very little practice but only the knowledge of recognizing and executing the shot.

Chapter Thirteen, Deflection, Squirt, Cling, Throw and Skid 209

If you are going to use english, you must understand these problem areas of the game and how to compensate. Do you know why the professionals have far fewer problems with this area than the average pool player? This chapter fully explains these principles.

Chapter Fourteen, The Ten Winning Rules for Nine Ball 223

If you play Nine Ball, these rules are a must. Following these 10 simple rules will raiseyour Nine Ball winning percentage. GUARANTEED!

About the Author 226

Acknowledgments

Although this book is the culmination of many years of learning, playing, and teaching the game of pool, no teaching book can be written without input from many authoritative and knowledgeable people. I would especially like to thank the pool and billiard instructors who helped me with the book—Wayne Norcross, Calvin Coker, and Roy Yamane. In fact, Roy is one of a select few Billiard Congress of America Master Instructors.

I would also like to thank two of my sparring partners for the past 10 years—Fernando "The Razor" Rivas and Ron "The Jump Master" Sakahara. If a ball can be jumped, Ron can do it. If a ball can be cut, Fernie can do it. These two never cease to amaze me at what they can do on a pool table.....I would also like to thank Joe Baggio for his business acumen and Allen Murdock for his technical assistance in bringing this book to fruition. And finally I would like to thank my wife, Nancy, for prodding me to slow down and do something I enjoy. I have truly enjoyed this project. I hope you enjoy reading and learning from this book. See you on the table, at an Expo, or in a tournament.

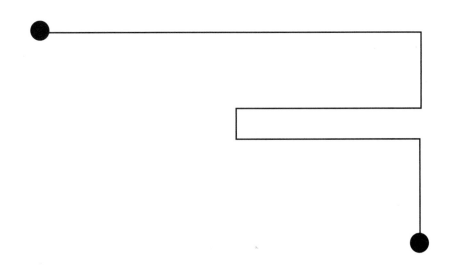

Chapter One
The Stroke Builders

BODY POSITION

A smooth relaxed stroke is mandatory if you are going to improve your game. One of the most overlooked and important parts of the stroke is your body position. Most players go from shot to shot by walking too close around the table. It has been said that a high percentage of missed shots is caused by improper body position.

Each shot should be approached from several feet beyond the table. Lightly hold the butt end of your cue at your hip and line up the shot with your bridge hand at about waist level using your entire peripheral field of vision. Then slowly approach the table in a straight line. Now lower your bridge hand and place it on the table about 12-16 inches in front of the cue ball (when possible) and slide it forward on the cloth towards the cue ball to about a normal 6-8 inch bridge distance.

The key to this set up is to be sure your right foot (left for left handed players) only moves directly forward on your approach to the table. This foot is of course attached to your leg that is attached to the hip where your initial aiming started with your hand at the hip holding the butt of your cue stick. Any movement left or right on your approach will cause a misalignment. If you get down on the shot and it does not look right, DO NOT try to correct the alignment by moving your arm in or out. Just step back from the table and start the approach set up all over again.

Alignment problems usually occur when your leg or hip is up against the table. Example - as you approach the table from the long rail side for a close to the rail cut shot and you have to "reach" to the cue ball, the natural tendency is for your hip to slide down the rail as you stretch. Now you are out of your original alignment. Also always shoot with both feet flat on the floor. When both feet are not on the floor, your body position is almost always out of alignment. Always use the bridge or cue extender for these shots. On those rare exception shots when only one foot is on the floor and you cannot use a mechanical helper, make sure your stomach is flat on the table. The table creates a stable base to hold your body in a balanced center position. But of course keeping your cue ball out of the "dead zone" discussed in Chapter 11 will keep you away from these out of alignment body position shots. Notice how seldom the professionals ever use a mechanical bridge. They know where their "dead zone" is on the table.

There has been a misconception for years that the butt of the cue must be held a couple of inches behind the balance point. The balance point of the cue stick has nothing to do with where the cue stick is held. With a few exceptions, you should always hold the cue where your forearm is perpendicular to the cue stick. This position can change slightly from shot to shot. Shorter players will normally hold the cue farther up the wrap and taller players farther down. If you are really tall or have long arms, you will probably need a little longer cue stick (59 - 60 inches).

THE STROKE

Randy Goettlicher at CUE TECH BILLIARD ACADEMY teaches what I think is the best stroking technique around. He calls this the SET, PAUSE, and FINISH. What this basically means is after you are in position and have taken several warm up strokes and are satisfied with your alignment, then you are SET. To proceed with the shot, slowly bring your cue stick back and PAUSE for 1-2 seconds. The simple theory here is that you have two main muscles in your arm that work opposite of each other. One must be at rest and receiving no impulses from the brain while the other is receiving impulses and working. If both muscles are trying to receive impulses, a smooth stroke is compromised. If you do not think this works, just watch Allison Fisher play. She is one of the top women professionals and has used this technique for years.

The final segment of the stroke is the FINISH. It does no good to do everything right up to this point and forget to finish properly. The finish consists of a nice smooth forward stroke using a loose back hand grip that accelerates the cue stick several inches past the cue ball. Your back hand should end up hitting your chest. This physical barrier is what limits your follow through and stops the stroke. Your entire body (especially your head) should now be frozen in the FINISH position for 1-2 seconds.

The following drills are designed to work on various segments of your stroke. It is necessary to develop a good stroke first before you can learn the other aspects of the game. Practice each of these often, and I guarantee your stroke will improve dramatically.

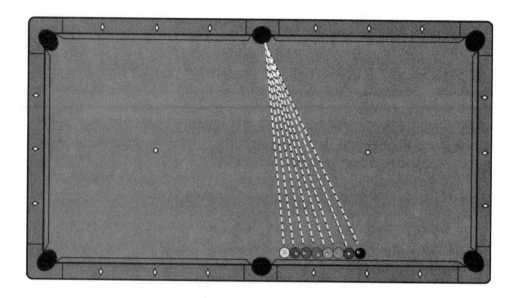

THE RHYTHM AND WRIST DRILL

This is an excellent drill for improving your stroke and wrist action. Place as many balls along the side rail cushion as the side pocket will hold beginning about 2 inches up from the side pocket. Then starting with the ball closest to the side pocket, shoot them in rapid succession into the opposite side pocket across the table. Begin at about one ball per second. If you are able to pocket all the balls consistently without miscuing, then begin to increase your speed. You will need to "shuffle" your feet slightly as you move up the side rail. Your whole body must move to stay in line with each shot.

As you become proficient at this drill, you should be able to pocket 8–10 balls in less than 5 seconds. Your stance will need to be more upright and both your bridge hand and grip hand will need to be very loose and flexible. This speed drill can only be accomplished accurately if your whole body is very loose. It is not a power drill but more a finesse drill. I suggest you use no chalk since you will be striking the balls with a center ball hit and chalk will only make the balls dirty.

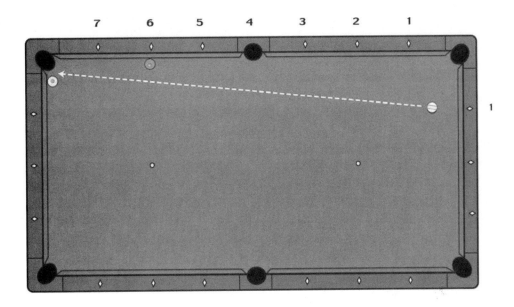

THE SET, PAUSE, AND FINISH DRILL

This drill will lay the foundation for your stroke. Repetitive practice of this drill will install the muscle memory techniques virtually needed for all shots. Place an object ball frozen to the end rail cushion just outside the pocket and another object ball at about diamond #6 against the side rail cushion. Now place a striped ball at the diamond #1 location on the other end rail about 4 inches off the cushion. Position the stripe on the ball facing the pocket. Now approach the table from behind, take several warm up strokes, and get in your SET position. Ask yourself if you are inline. Is your grip hand loose and your arm perpendicular to the cue stick? If everything looks and feels ok, then pull the cue stick back and PAUSE for 1-2 seconds. Finally, accelerate the cue stick smoothly forward striking the ball slightly above center to give it forward roll. The cue stick should continue forward past where the striped ball was for several inches. Remember your chest stops the cue stick and not your arm. Now you are in the FINISH position. Freeze and hold this position for 1-2 seconds and evaluate the shot. The stripe on the ball should rotate only in the direction of the pocket (no side spin) and the ball should be pocketed missing the other object balls. Repeat this exercise for all 7 striped balls.

Once you become proficient, begin to move the side rail cushion object ball down closer to the pocket. Now the opening begins to become even smaller requiring even more accuracy. How far down can you move this ball and still pocket the striped ball?

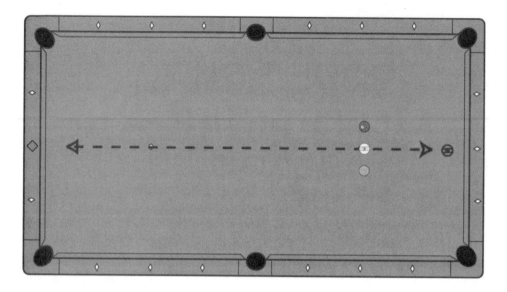

THE CENTER BALL HIT DRILL

Most players fail to contact the cue ball with the cue tip at the center. Striking the cue ball away from its perpendicular center axis can cause the intended path of the cue ball to be altered. This will be discussed at length in Chapter 13. This drill is the best at developing that true center ball hit.

Place a striped ball on the spot with the stripe pointed directly at the middle diamond on the end rail. Now place a solid object ball on each side of the striped ball about 1 ball width apart. This will give about a three ball width opening. Place a chalk cube directly over this middle end rail diamond to give you a better aiming point. Have one of the corners of the chalk pointed directly at the striped ball. Shoot the striped ball slightly above center to give it forward roll directly at the chalk. This ball should rotate with the stripe on the ball remaining parallel to the side rails. It should then rebound off the rail cushion and return between the two solid object balls.

If the stripe rotates off center, the usual cause is the cue tip striking the ball to the side of its center axis. If the stripe on the ball rotates parallel to the side rails but the ball does not go between the solid balls, the usual cause is missing the aiming point. As you become more proficient at this shot, begin to increase the speed. And as you become better yet, move the solid balls slightly closer together.

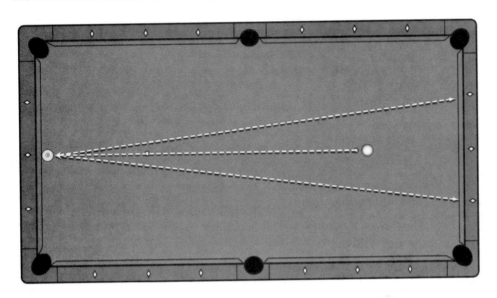

THE AIMING DRILL

This drill is very similar to the previous illustration. Here you place the cue ball on the spot and another object ball frozen to the end rail cushion at the middle diamond. Now stroke the cue ball one tip below the perpendicular center axis with a moderate stroke. Aim directly at the object ball. If the object ball is hit perfectly solid, the cue ball will rebound straight back to the middle diamond at the other end of the table. This is much harder than it looks. Just getting the cue ball back between the two outside diamonds is considered a successful execution.

Sometimes finding the center of the cue ball is easier on the draw stroke than the follow stroke. If you start your aiming with the cue tip on the cloth directly underneath the edge of the cue ball, you can actually see the reflection of the tip on the cue ball from the lights over the table. If you place the cue tip under the edge of the cue ball and move it from side to side, you will notice the reflection on the cue ball moves right with it. This is why many of the professionals start their warm up strokes with the cue tip on the cloth under the edge of the cue ball. Once they determine they are inline with center ball, they will move the tip to the desired english location. This drill will also begin to teach you the draw stroke necessary for some of the later chapters.

While these first several drills can be boring, they will begin to establish the beginning of your stroke. If you are unable to attain a consistent desired result, I suggest you contact a professional instructor for advice.

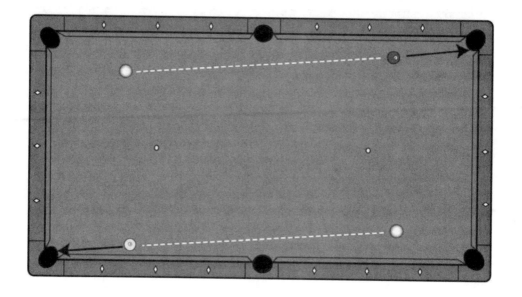

THE #1 STROKE BUILDER - THE STOP SHOT

Bert Kinister in one of his teaching videos says, "this shot is the most important shot in pool and will create a stroke where there is no stroke." I could not agree more. Set the shot up with the object ball about 1 diamond from the end rail and the cue ball 1 diamond from the other end rail and lined up straight into the corner pocket. The goal here is to pocket the object ball and to stop the cue ball or allow it to roll slightly forward and replace where the object ball was. It requires a very level stroke and a slightly below dead center cue ball hit. The key to this shot is the speed the cue ball is hit. The cue ball must strike the object ball while it is "sliding" so all of its energy can be transferred to the object ball. If the speed is too slow, the cue ball will pick up forward roll and follow the object ball. If it is hit too low and too fast, the cue ball will still be spinning backwards on contact with the object ball and draw back from the object ball.

This shot needs to be practiced at every practice routine in order to develop a consistent stroke. Just approach the table from several feet back, go through the SET, PAUSE, and FINISH routine and execute the shot. Consistent runs of 25 without a miss and an occasional run of 50-100 balls should be your goal. If at the beginning, you are unable to attain these numbers, move the balls a little closer together. I also suggest you set the shot up on both sides of the table. This will allow you to continuously shoot while walking around the table.

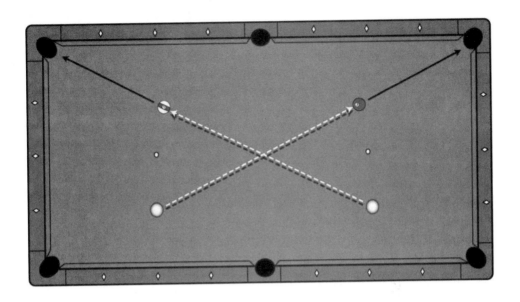

THE #2 STROKE BUILDER

This shot is very similar to the previous illustration but the pocket will play slightly larger. Here you are able to see the full "mouth" of the pocket. Set the shot up straight into the pocket. I learned the following suggestion from BCA Certified Master Level Instructor Roy Yamane years ago for all consistent set ups. Stretch a string from corner center pocket to corner center pocket and place the Avery™ white "donut" reinforcements directly under the string line where you want the balls positioned. Place the balls along this string line about two diamonds up from each end and one diamond in from the side rail. This will give you consistent ball placement each time.

The goal is to pocket the ball and stop the cue ball or possibly let it drift slightly towards the side rail. This is called playing the "pro" side of the pocket. If you allow the cue ball to drift towards the center of the table, the object ball will go more to the unforgiving side of the pocket. If the object ball contacts any part of the side rail cushion, it will normally be missed. However, if 50% or less of the object ball contacts the end rail side of the corner pocket, it will usually go in. This shot comes up quite often in nine ball on the big tables. Practicing this shot will give you confidence when those occasions arise.

Again set this shot up on both sides of the table to allow for easier continuous play. Approach the table for several feet back and do not let the corner of the table interfere with your proper body alignment position. Consistent runs of 25 or more in a row without a miss should be your goal.

9

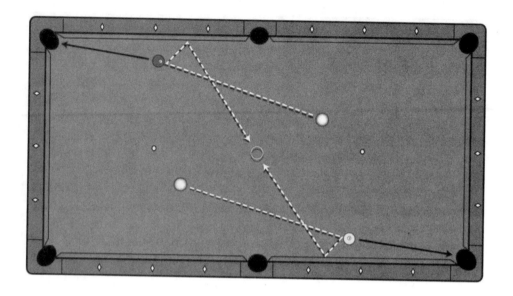

THE MOST COMMON SHOT IN 9 BALL

The goal here is to pocket the object ball into the corner pocket and bring the cue ball back to the center of the table. This shot comes up time and time again when playing 9 ball. This shot will begin to give you a feel for your cue ball control. This topic will be discussed at length in Chapter 11. Set the shot up as illustrated and use a moderate to firm loose stroke with about 1/2 tip of low english. Again use the white "donuts" to replicate the same shot each time. Once you attain consistent success, duplicate the shot on the other side of the table. Notice how on one side of the table you are stretching a little to reach the cue ball and your leg or hip is up against the end of the table. If you are missing this shot, it is probably due to improper body placement. Remember at the beginning of this chapter, I discussed the importance of proper alignment and body position. This is one of the most common shots where body position can be affected by the table. If you get down on the shot and it does not look right or does not feel right, then just back away from the table and start the set up process all over again.

Practice this shot often. Have you ever noticed how the professionals always seem to bring the cue ball back to the center of the table whenever possible? This way they usually have a good solid bridge placement area and the table does not hinder their proper body alignment. Also even on the nine foot tables, all shots are within 4 feet from this middle table position.

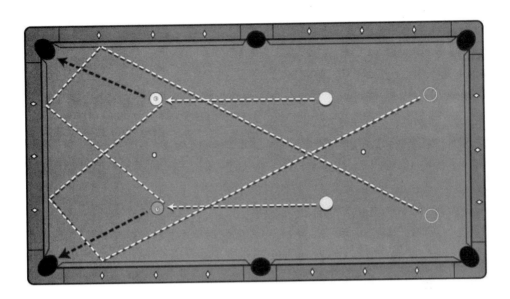

THE SECOND MOST COMMON SHOT IN 9 BALL

This shot again comes up very often. Place both the cue ball and object ball one diamond out from the side cushion rail with the object ball at the diamond #6 and the cue ball at the diamond #3. Begin shooting the object ball in softly with about 1 tip of high english (top spin). While the previous drill showed you the effects of low english (draw), this drill will begin to teach you follow english. As your pocketing skills increase, begin to add more speed. If this shot is hit hard enough, it is almost a dead scratch 2 rails to the corner pocket. You should become proficient enough at this shot to make the object ball and stop the cue ball about 12-18 inches from this corner pocket.

Set this shot up from both sides of the table as illustrated. You will be surprised how each of these shots appear quite different. In fact, if you practice one side for 10-15 minutes, you will probably begin to miss this shot at first when you go to the other side. Your brain is still thinking about the previous shot because it has seen it so many times in a row. Also always remember to shoot towards the "pro" side or the more forgiving side of the pocket. Any contact of the object ball with the side rail cushion first almost always results in a miss. Your aiming point is always towards the end rail side of the pocket (center of the pocket opening).

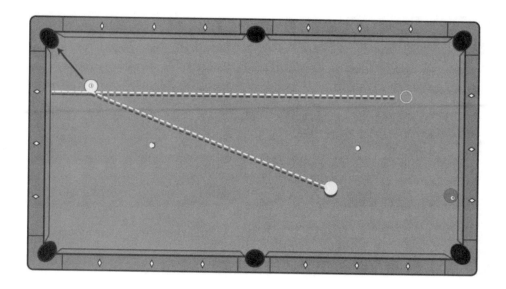

THE LONG RAIL FOLLOW SHOT

This shot is designed to improve your perpendicular centerline high english follow stroke. Place the object ball one diamond in from the end rail and one diamond in from the side rail. Now place the cue ball at the other end of the table two diamonds in from the end rail and one diamond in from the side rail. This shot is a little more difficult than the previous shots as there is more distance between the cue ball and the object ball. Second, a more forceful stroke is needed for proper cue ball position. Stroke the cue ball slightly above center with a firm stroke. Since the cue ball will travel almost six feet before it contacts the object ball, it will pick up its own forward roll (top spin).

The object ball should be pocketed into the corner pocket and the cue ball should follow forward, rebounding off the end rail cushion straight up the table towards position on the next object ball. If you make the object ball and the cue ball contacts the side rail cushion, you inadvertently applied some right english to the cue ball. If you make the object ball but your cue ball comes up on the short side (close to the bottom side rail) of the next object ball, you applied some left english to the cue ball. Only a centerline hit on the cue ball will bring the cue ball straight back up the table for position on the next shot.

It is amazing how often the side pockets get in the way of the rebounding cue ball when side english is also applied to the cue ball. The key to this shot is a firm smooth good follow through stroke. You must have this shot in your repertoire if you play nine ball on the large 4 1/2 x 9 ft. tables.

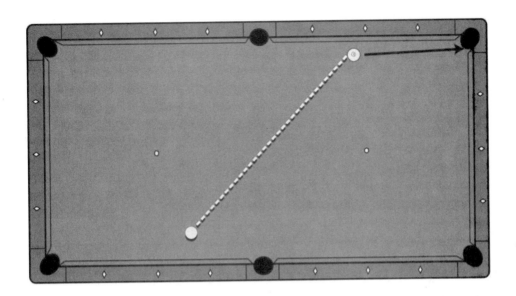

THE SIDE RAIL CUT SHOT

Many players have a very difficult time executing this type of a thin cut angle shot. Set the shot up with the object ball less than one inch from the side rail cushion and at about the 2 1/2 diamond mark. Now place the cue ball on the other side of the table at about the 5 1/2 diamond mark and about 8-10 inches out from the cushion as illustrated. Virtually the edge of the cue ball must strike the edge of the object ball to pocket it into the corner pocket. Use a moderate center ball hit on the cue ball and it will rebound straight across the table. The key to this shot is actually determining the opening of the pocket. Set the shot up as illustrated using the white donut reinforcements. Now stand directly behind the corner pocket where the object ball will be pocketed. Notice how the "jaws" of the pocket open up towards the middle of the table. Now move to the end rail and sight the object ball to the pocket. Notice how the width of the pocket is reduced by about one inch. The opening becomes smaller and the margin for error is greater. There is a right way and a wrong way to shoot this shot.

If the object ball is allowed to strike the side rail cushion on the way towards the pocket, in most cases it will either rattle in the jaws or rebound towards the center of the table leaving an easy shot for your opponent. However, if the aiming point is moved towards the end rail side of the pocket, the object ball will either be pocketed or will rebound off the end rail cushion back to the side rail. Now your opponent must either bank or play safe. The goal is to not allow this object ball to contact the side rail cushion.

Chapter Two
The Practice Shots

These practice shots are designed to reinforce what you learned in Chapter 1. You must learn both the theory and execution of these shots for other chapters in this book. Some are fairly easy while others will take some time to learn. The illustrations will concentrate on the stop shot, follow shot, draw shot, rail shot, and stun shot. I have some words of caution. DO NOT forget about the STROKE BUILDERS in Chapter 1. They must first be mastered before you can get a high percentage of execution on these shots.

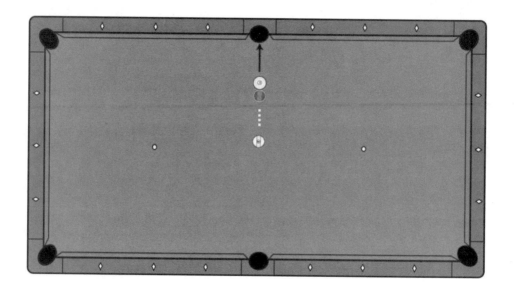

THE STOP SHOT

This drill is intended to teach you both the theory and execution of the stop shot. Place a solid object ball close to the side pocket with a striped object ball at about the center of the table as illustrated. The shot should be lined up straight into the side pocket. Stretch a string between the centers of the side pockets. Now place the white donut reinforcements under the string to get a consistent straight in ball placement shot. Have the number on the striped object ball facing straight up as shown.

Now shoot the striped ball at the solid ball with a dead center ball hit and a medium to firm stroke. Use no chalk as this will dirty the object ball and chalk is not necessary for a center cue ball hit. The solid ball should be pocketed and the striped ball should stop with the number still pointing straight up. This is because the striped ball first actually "slides" across the cloth before it picks up any forward roll. Upon contact with the solid object ball, all of the energy from the striped ball is released into the solid ball causing the striped ball to stop. If the striped ball rolls forward after contact, it was either hit too slowly, allowing it to pick up forward roll after it quit sliding, or the striped ball was contacted slightly above center with the cue tip.

If the striped ball moves to one side or the other after contact, the solid ball was hit slightly off center. And if the striped ball spins in either direction after contact, it was contacted by the cue tip of the cue stick slightly off to the side. Practice this drill often. It will give you immediate feedback on determining center ball.

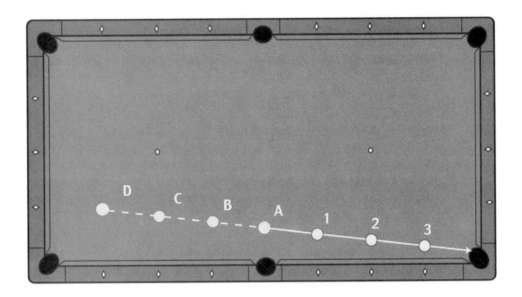

THE DRAW STROKE

This is the best exercise at developing the draw stroke. Start with the cue ball at position "A" and the object ball at position #1. Practice drawing the cue ball back to positions, A, B, C, & D. Once this is mastered, place the object ball at position #2 and again draw back to positions A, B, C, & D. Then move the object ball to position #3 and repeat the same process again. The next sequences begin to get much harder. Now place the cue ball at position "B" and repeat the entire sequence again. Repeat again with the cue ball at position "C". Once you have reached position "D" with the cue ball and are able to accurately complete the drill sequence, you are ready for the professional tour.

The main key to the draw stroke is a very loose back hand grip. This stroke seems to cause more "clinching" and "death grips" on the cue stick than any other stroke. You will have a very hard time drawing the cue ball with a tight grip. Second, move your bridge hand slightly closer to the cue ball. This will reduce shaft vibration (increasing accuracy) on these low hits on the cue ball and allow for an extended follow through. Also don't forget to move your back hand slightly forward to keep your forearm perpendicular to the cue stick. And last, always contact the cue ball about one tip below center and only vary the cue ball speed depending on how far you want the cue ball to come back. By only varying the speed of the cue ball and keeping the cue ball hit constant, the draw distance control can be learned much easier. Don't get discouraged as this drill is much harder than it looks.

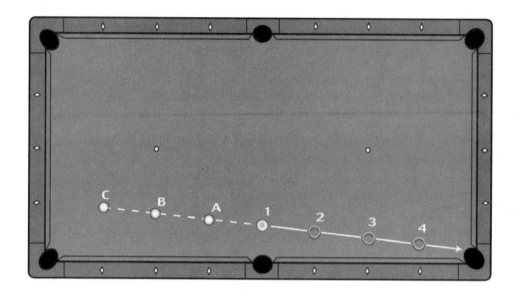

THE FOLLOW SHOT

This drill is almost the same as the draw shot drill except the cue ball is now moving forward. Following the cue ball to a desired location after contact with the object ball is always easier than drawing the cue ball. Whenever you have ball-in-hand and multiple pockets available, always follow the cue ball for position on the next shot. Again, place the cue ball at position "A" and an object ball at position "#1". Practice pocketing the object ball and follow the cue ball to positions #2, #3, & #4. Once this is mastered, repeat the same sequence again with the cue ball at position "B". And finally, move the cue ball to position "C". This position is the hardest as it involves greater distances between the cue ball and object ball locations. At position #4, it is always better to end up slightly short versus going too far (the deadly scratch).

As you can see, the follow shot is like the draw shot in that speed and cue tip position-ing determine the roll of the cue ball. Keep the cue tip position constant (about one tip above the perpendicular center line axis) and vary the speed only for the desired follow cue ball position. By varying both the speed and cue tip contact point on the cue ball (two variables), it is more difficult to learn and obtain the "feel" needed for the desired follow cue ball control. Again, I would like to repeat what I said before. Whenever you have a choice between follow or draw to obtain the same desired cue ball position, always use follow.

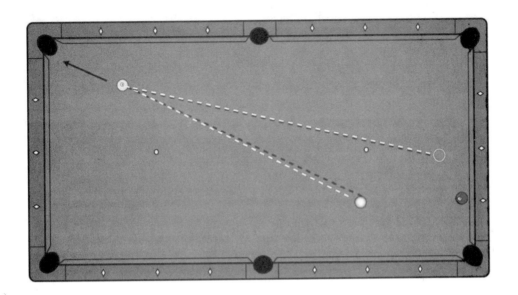

THE POWER DRAW SHOT

This is absolutely one of the most difficult shots in pool. Set the shot up as illustrated. This power draw shot requires the cue ball to travel great distances accurately to the object ball while spinning backwards the whole time. After contact with the object ball, the cue ball must then back up essentially on the same path it arrived to the desired position spot on the table. The following points should help you learn the execution of this shot:

- Relax your **entire** body including your bridge hand and forearm and especially your grip hand.

- **Shorten** your bridge to about 5-6 inches from the cue ball and move your grip hand up to remain perpendicular to the cue stick.

- Be sure you are hitting the cue ball about 1 1/2 cue tips below center and directly on **centerline**. Start your warm up strokes with the cue tip on the cloth and verify you are on the centerline of the cue ball by the reflection of the cue tip on the base of the cue ball.

- Use a **very loose, firm** stroke. Do not "baby" this shot. It is almost like you are throwing the stick through the cue ball.

- **Snap** your wrist upon contact with the cue ball. Many of the professionals can draw the cue ball great distances with a very loose snap action wrist motion and very little arm movement.

- Use an **extended** follow through of 12-16 inches. This exaggerated follow through keeps clinching to a minimum.

19

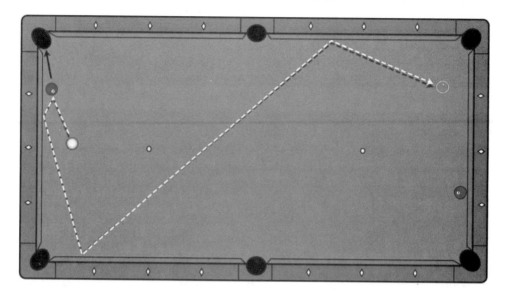

THE THREE RAIL POWER DRAW SHOT

Here you are almost straight in on the object ball and must get all the way up to the other end of the table for position on the next shot. The object here is to impart both bottom spin and side spin on the cue ball. This will allow the cue ball to come backwards after contact with the object ball and the side spin will widen the rebound angle off the cushion. Use the same firm loose snap extra follow through stroke discussed in the previous illustration and strike the cue ball in the lower left quadrant with your cue tip. You will need more draw spin than side spin as the cushion will impart more side spin on the drawing cue ball. Proper execution will have the cue ball drawing three rails to the other end of the table. One key to this shot is to be sure the object ball does not contact the end rail cushion. Because this shot is executed with a very forceful stroke, the object ball must go cleanly into the pocket or it will "rattle" away from the pocket. Be sure to aim at the center of the pocket opening.

This is an excellent shot to try "back hand" english. This area will be discussed at length later in Chapter 13. Basically what you do here is line up the shot with a center ball hit with about a 6 inch bridge. On your last warm up stroke, move the cue tip to the lower left quadrant of the cue ball by "swaying your body". Do not move your bridge hand. Now pull the cue stick back, pause, and firmly stroke through the cue ball. Again, the cue ball should draw three rails to the other end of the table.

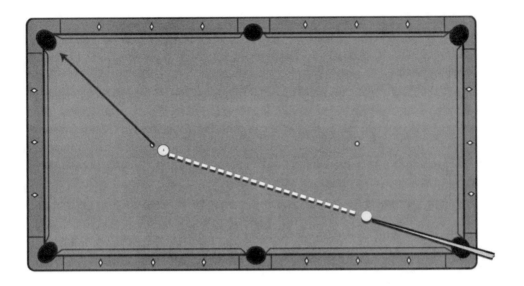

THE SPOT SHOT

This is one of the most common shots in many games of pool. Here the object ball has been placed on the spot for various reasons and you have ball-in-hand behind the head string. You should have the same accuracy on this shot as a good basketball player (not Shaq) should have shooting a foul shot.

There are several methods to shoot this shot but I found the following one is the simplest. Place the cue ball just behind the head string line. Line the cue ball up between the center of the back corner pocket and the spotted ball. Now aim for a 1/2 ball hit on the object ball with a slightly above (less slide) dead center ball hit on the cue ball. Another way to phrase this is to aim the cue tip at the edge of the object ball. Since the cue tip is aimed at the center of the cue ball, a one half ball movement on the object ball would have the cue tip extending to the edge of the object ball.

The butt end of the cue stick should go over the center of the back corner pocket. Use a moderate loose good follow through stroke. Also always aim slightly to the end rail side of the pocket. Sometimes if the object ball is missed towards the end rail side, it can go two rails into the back corner pocket. Be careful of this shot if you are shooting the eight ball in a call shot eight ball game. With practice, you should be able to make 10-15 in a row without a miss.

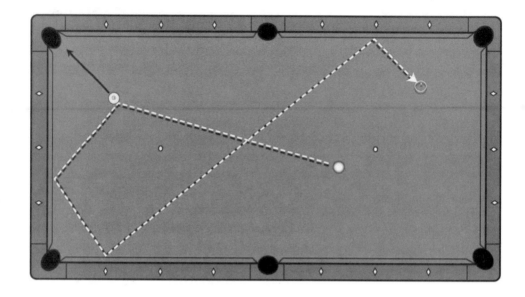

THE NATURAL 3 RAIL SHAPE SHOT

This is another very common shot that comes up in many different types of pool games. This shot will begin to familiarize you with the tangent line and the speed necessary to get the cue ball to travel three rails for position. The most common mistake on this shot is thinking that high english will be necessary on the cue ball to get it to travel towards the other end of the table.

This follow english will invariably cause the cue ball to go three rails into the corner pocket. The follow english will narrow the carom angle of the cue ball to the end rail cushion and the cushions will impart spin on the cue ball forcing it into the direction of the corner pocket. Go back to the shot on page 10. See how the cue ball path is directly into the corner pocket.

The proper way to shoot this shot is with a firm dead center cue ball hit. The cue ball will carom off the object ball along the tangent line and proceed three rails to position on the next object ball at the other end of the table. This wider line negates any possibility of a scratch into the corner pocket.

On all shots when there is distance between the cue ball and object ball and a firm stroke is necessary, you are always better off hitting the cue ball closest to the center along its perpendicular centerline axis to give it its truest roll.

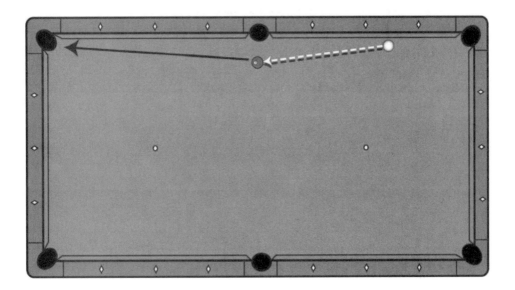

THE WRONG SIDE OF THE OBJECT BALL SHOT

Here if you could have controlled your cue ball better, you would have had a very easy shot into the side pocket or a straight in shot to the corner. Although the shot does not look that difficult, it is one of the most missed shots in pool. The key to this shot is just like the thin cut shot in Chapter 1. Your aiming point is towards the outside of the pocket.

If the object ball hits the side rail cushion on the way towards the pocket, it usually will rattle in the "jaws" or rebound away staying close to the pocket. On the other hand, if the object ball misses towards the end rail cushion (the pro side), it will roll back up the side rail leaving a bank or a return safety. If this ball is stroked firmly and is missed on the end rail side, it even has a chance to be banked one rail back to the corner pocket.

Shoot this shot with a center ball hit on the cue ball. Be careful as high english can cause the cue ball to scratch into the opposite corner pocket.

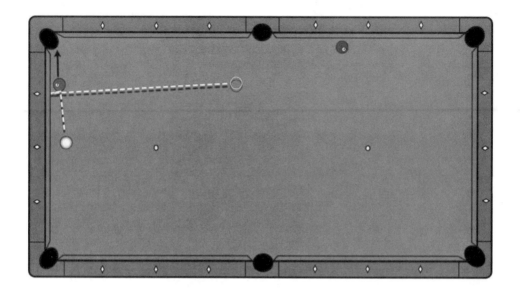

THE END RAIL POWER STUN SHOT

Here you violated rule #6 of "THE 10 WINNING RULES FOR 9 BALL". You are almost straight in on the object ball on the end rail cushion, and you must move the cue ball up the table for an easier shot on the next object ball. This shot is executed much like the break shot that will be discussed in Chapter 8.

Use a dead center ball hit with a very firm loose stroke. If you clinch your grip hand, the cue ball will only move several inches. On the other hand if you strike the cue ball "smartly" with a very loose grip and good fluid follow through, the cue ball will rebound straight off the rail several feet.

Another key to this shot is aiming towards the center of the pocket. Since the object ball is being hit with great force, any contact with the end rail cushion will cause it to be rejected by the pocket. As you become more proficient at this shot using a firm loose fluid stroke, you will notice you will need less force to move the cue ball several feet.

This is an excellent shot to set up as per the above illustration with the white donut reinforcements for a repetitive practice drill. You are using virtually the same stroke as the draw stroke except the cue ball is being hit dead center. Notice how the more rigid the wrist and tighter the grip, the cue ball moves the least no matter how hard you stroke the cue ball.

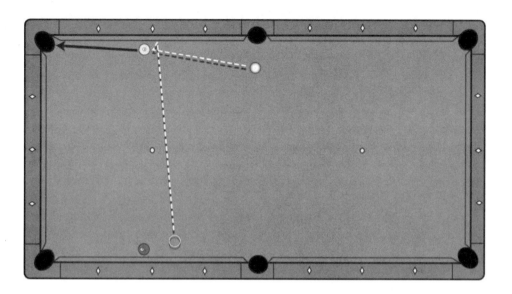

SIDE RAIL POWER STUN SHOT

This shot is very similar to the prior illustration. This time the object ball is slightly off the side rail and again there is only a slight angle to the cue ball. The cue ball is located just above the side pocket and about 1/2 diamond in from the side rail cushion. You must pocket this object ball and get the cue ball to the other side of the table for the next shot. I have repeated this shot as it comes up even more often than the previous shot. This shot is a little more difficult as you will have to stretch slightly to reach the cue ball and the object ball is farther from the pocket. The tendency is to drive the object ball into the side rail cushion. This is because your hip is up against the table causing your body to be out of proper alignment. Always step back from the table and reset a second time on this shot. Be cognizant of how much pressure the table has exerted on your lower body. The more pressure, the more your body is probably out of alignment. Because of the force of the shot, your body position cannot be compromised as this can greatly affect your accuracy. Again the aiming point is at the center of the pocket. If the object ball hits the side rail cushion on the way to the pocket, it will almost surely be missed. Execute the shot the same as the previous shot. The object ball should be pocketed into the corner pocket and the cue ball should rebound from the side rail cushion straight across the table towards the other side. Use the same center cue ball relaxed loose stroke. It is almost like "throwing" the cue stick at the cue ball.

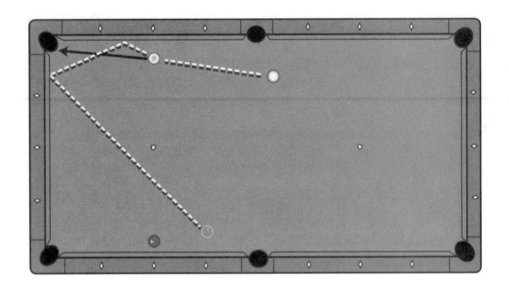

THE TWO RAIL SOFT FOLLOW SHOT

Here the previous set up is duplicated but you need to use a different way to position the cue ball for the next shot. Instead of using a lot of force, you just apply a lot of high left (running) english and shoot the cue ball softer. The high english will supply the forward roll and the left english will give the cue ball even more speed as it rebounds off the cushion. Since you are hitting the cue ball softly, you don't have to worry about the negative (deflection, squirt, etc.) factors that will be discussed in Chapter 13. Again aim for the center of the pocket and the cue ball will rebound off both the side and end cushion towards the next object ball.

I normally prefer this route versus the previous illustration as the softer shot and left english makes the pocket play a little "bigger". This is always the best route on a fast table. The previous page illustrated route is best on a slow table as the distance the cue ball must travel is less. And remember it never does any good to get great shape on the next ball unless you make the current object ball.

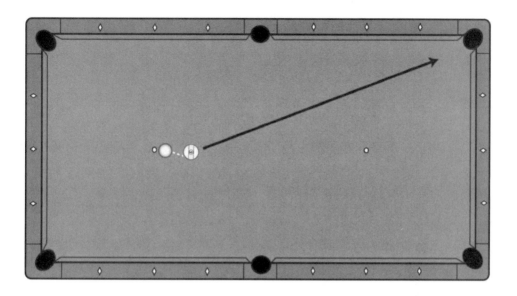

THE CLOSE TOGETHER SHOT

When the cue ball and object ball are very close together, it is very difficult to "see and feel" where to contact the object ball. These shots are sometimes more difficult than the long shots where there is great distance between the two balls. Set the two balls up about 2-3 inches apart and lined up towards the middle end rail diamond. Use a striped ball as it is easier to reference a contact point on a striped ball rather than a solid ball.

The first thing you want to do is align your cue stick over the center of the object ball with the cue tip on the cloth and pointed towards the center of the pocket where you want the object ball to go. This will give you a reference point on the back side of the object ball where it will need to be contacted by the cue ball. Now back away from the table and approach the shot from several feet back staring at this contact point on the object ball. Use a shorter than normal bridge and a high english hit on the cue ball. Also get down on your cue stick as low as possible. Your chin should virtually be touching the cue stick. This will allow you to see the cue ball, object ball, and the pocket without moving your head and with very little eye movement.

Your peripheral vision comes more into play on these shots than any other type of shot. Look at the cue ball, then the object ball, and then the pocket. Repeat this process several times. If you feel you are properly set, shoot the shot. If it does not look or feel right, don't shoot and start the entire set up process all over again.

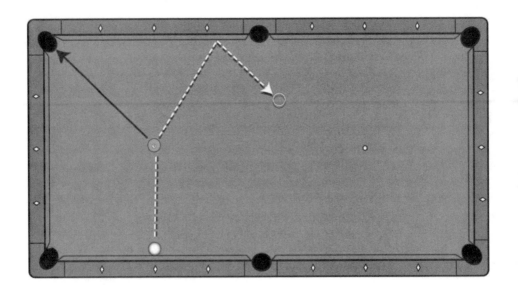

THE RAIL SHOT

Here again you have violated one of the "10 WINNING 9 BALL RULES" and left the cue ball against the rail cushion. Set the object ball on the spot and the cue ball frozen to the side rail cushion at the second diamond up from the corner pocket. A stable bridge that allows the cue stick to rest on the rail is crucial for this shot. This will help keep the cue stick as level as possible. There are several tendencies that occur on these shots. Most players seem to "punch" at the cue ball rather than stroke through the cue ball. Be sure to go through your normal SET, PAUSE, AND FINISH routine and stroke through the cue ball. The second tendency is to raise your head. Always concentrate on staying down on this shot as the FINISH is very important. You actually may want to get lower than normal on this shot.

The third tendency is to undercut the object ball. The positive aspect of this tendency is that it plays towards the forgiving (pro) side of the pocket. A miss on this side has the object ball rebounding off the side rail cushion leaving it along the end rail cushion. Too thin of a hit results in a sell out. The object ball will rebound off the end rail cushion leaving it close to the pocket along the side rail cushion.

Another tendency involves rail shots that are at about a 45 degree angle. The fingers holding the cue stick together have a tendency to move especially when force is used. On this shot, you will need to squeeze your fingers tightly against the cue stick to inhibit its sideways movement and shorten your bridge for better accuracy. Understanding the pitfalls on this shot will greatly improve your off-the-rail pocketing skills.

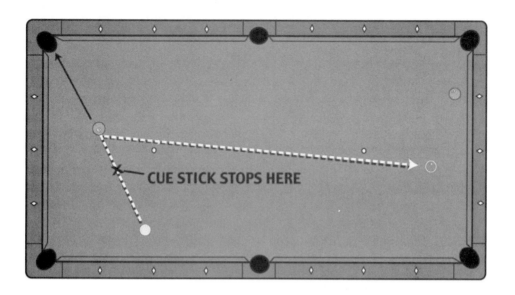

CUE STICK STOPS HERE

THE RAIL STUN DRAW SHOT

This shot requires the best stoke you can muster. Here you are almost straight in on the object ball and close to the rail but must get to the other end of the table for the next shot. Approach the table from behind but do not get as close as your normal stance. Now reach out with your bridge hand and form a closed rail bridge with your cue stick. Your front arm should be virtually straight. This will get as much of the cue stick in front of you as is physically possible. Now lower your body and get as low as possible over the cue stick. You want to use an extremely loose moderate to hard stroke and contact the cue ball about one tip below center. The cue stick will virtually drop through your bridge hand to the cloth and continue along the cloth for 6-8 inches.

After contact with the object ball, the cue ball will first "stun" slightly forward and to the right. This will create a new tangent line angle for the rebounding cue ball to draw towards the other end of the table. The key to this shot is a very loose grip hand and an exaggerated follow through. Don't get discouraged on this shot if you have trouble with the execution. It is one of the toughest shots in the book but is excellent at building a stroke. Also this shot is a little tough on the cloth. Be sure your tip is nicely rounded and has no rough edges.

Chapter Three
Safety Play

As your skills improve, safety play is needed to take your game to the next level. When playing a high caliber player, improper execution of a good safety usually results in loss of the game. The best safeties are where both the cue ball and object ball are hidden behind other blocker balls. This means your opponent will have to kick at the ball using multiple rails. This usually results with ball-in-hand for you unless your opponent knows the secrets discussed and illustrated in Chapter 4.

When left with a tough layout on the table, sometimes it is better to run several balls and play a good safety. It is sometimes better to "FOLD" (play a safety) them than to "HOLD" (shoot a low percentage shot) them. Hopefully, you will get ball-in-hand which will allow for a much easier chance for a run out or play another good safety. Now your opponent is really getting frustrated!

In all my years, I can count on one hand the number of times I have seen a player (even the good ones) practice safety play. Safety play does not come naturally. It usually requires moving both the cue ball and the object ball to specific spots on the table. It requires knowledge of the "Tangent Line" discussed in Chapter 7 and cue ball positioning discussed in Chapter 9. Practice these safeties often. The simple safeties should be mastered fairly quickly. Then after reading and understanding Chapters 7 & 9, come back to this chapter and you will find execution of the more difficult safeties has become much easier.

Practice the following safeties and you will be amazed how your winning percentage improves. Also always remember rules #3 & #8 of my 10 WINNING RULES FOR 9 BALL.

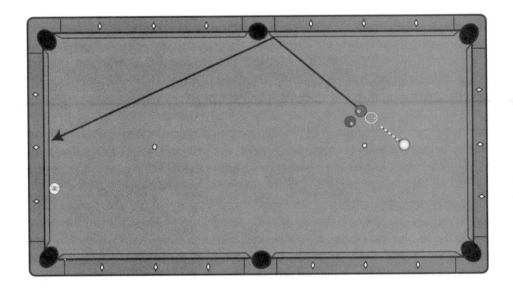

THE SIMPLEST SAFETY

This is the simplest of all safeties. All you have to do here is execute a simple stop shot that you learned in Chapters 1 & 2. You do not have to be concerned where the object ball goes (although towards the middle and away from the rail is better) as long as it remains at the other end of the table. The concentration here is on the cue ball and a dead center hit on the object ball. Remember the cue ball must "slide" to the object ball in order to transfer all of its energy and stop. This is normally accomplished with a dead center cue ball hit and a moderate stroke. If this moderate stroke will cause the object ball to rebound back towards the other end of the table, hit the cue ball a little slower but with a little low english. Now the cue ball will spin backwards for several inches before it begins to slide. Any forward roll or backwards spin on the cue ball at contact with the object ball will cause it to move away from behind this blocker ball.

This shot can also be an offensive weapon when playing 9 ball. Presume your opponent has just given you ball-in-hand. Your first inclination is to start running balls. However, the better percentage play oftentimes is to locate the nine ball on the table and play another safety. Now position the cue ball where you can hit the object ball next to the 9 ball and leave the cue ball behind an obstructer ball. If your opponent fails to make a legal hit, you may have ball-in-hand again and an easy combination on the 9 ball. Or if you fail to position the object properly for an easy combination on the nine ball, you may want to execute another safety.

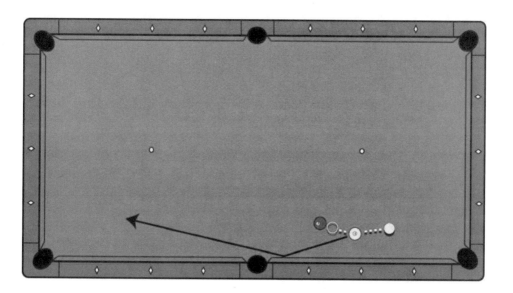

THE ROLL UP SAFETY

This is another simple safety. Here again, the object ball is close to a potential obstructer ball. The goal is to hit the object ball towards the other end of the table and let the cue ball "drift" directly behind the obstructer ball. The closer you can get the cue ball to the blocker ball, the more angles that will be cut off for your opponent to use to kick at the object ball. The two keys are to first determine the tangent line (discussed in detail in Chapter 7) needed for the path the cue ball must go to end up directly behind the blocker ball after contact with the object ball.

Second, the proper speed necessary to position the object ball and the amount of high english applied to the cue ball must be determined. These shots are finesse shots that require a shorter bridge and back stroke. Also many players fail to take their normal warm up strokes on this shot. Treat this shot no differently than any other shot. Your goal is to actually have the cue ball rest up against the obstructer ball. Even if the cue ball strikes the obstructer ball, it is normally going so slowly that the obstructer ball will only move 1-2 inches forward while still blocking the path to the object ball. Also try to position the object ball away from the rail towards the middle of the table. The object ball at this position is much more difficult to kick at and hit. An object ball left close to the rail is easier to kick at because if it is missed directly by the cue ball, it may be contacted after rebounding from the cushion.

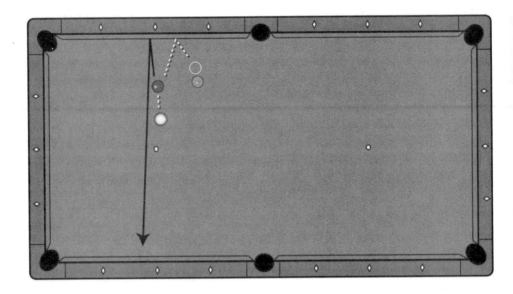

THE INSIDE ENGLISH KILL SAFETY

This safety comes up quite often in all games of pool. The goal here is to bank the object ball directly across to the other side of the table and to leave the cue ball behind a blocker ball. This is accomplished by applying extreme inside (in this case left hand) english to the cue ball and striking the object ball slightly off center. This inside english accomplishes two things. First, it imparts the opposite english on the object ball. So even though the object ball strikes the cushion at an angle, it will rebound off the cushion virtually straight across the table due to the opposite english pick up from the cue ball. Second, the inside english applied to the cue ball will "kill" the cue ball as it rebounds from the cushion causing it to drift slightly behind the blocker ball.

Practice this safety often. Use the white donut reinforcements to obtain consistent shot set up. Once you become proficient at this shot, remove the donuts and vary the ball placement. Experiment with different amounts of english, speed, and contact points until you obtain the desired results. Remember this is a finesse shot. Use a shorter bridge and back stroke and always take several warm up strokes to acquire the proper "feel" for this shot. It is always very important to move the object ball close to the other side rail cushion so if you fail to hide the cue ball behind the blocker ball, your opponent is still only left with a difficult bank shot or an extremely difficult cut shot.

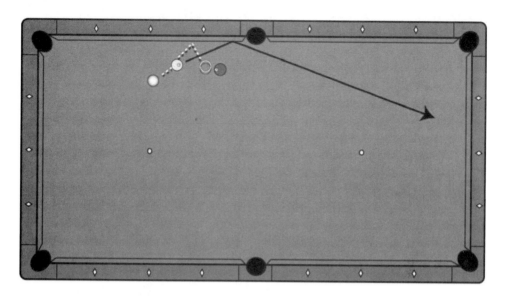

THE RUNNING ENGLISH RAIL SAFTEY

This safety is a combination of the previous two safeties. Your goal is to hit the object ball towards the end rail and leave the cue ball behind the blocker ball. Here you use both follow and side spin to position the cue ball behind the blocker ball. You first must determine where the cue ball must contact the cushion to rebound behind the blocker ball. Then you determine the rebound tangent line path the cue ball will take after striking the object ball to arrive at this point. Remember both the follow and side spin (the running english) will widen the rebound angle of the cue ball off the object ball and the cushion.

Stroke the cue ball with a soft stroke and a little high right english. The object ball will go to the other end of the table and the cue ball will rebound off the side rail cushion behind the blocker ball. This safety is a little more difficult than the roll up safety, so I suggest you try to position the object ball on the end rail. This way if you miss the "hook" behind the blocker ball, your opponent is left with a difficult bank or a return safety. Once you gain confidence in these safeties, leave the object ball more towards the center of the table away from the end rail cushion. This will leave a much more difficult kick shot for your opponent. Again this is another finesse shot. Use a short bridge and back stroke with several warm up strokes to obtain the proper feel for the shot. Use the white donuts to replicate the shot. Once you obtain consistency in the execution, remove the donuts and vary the ball placements.

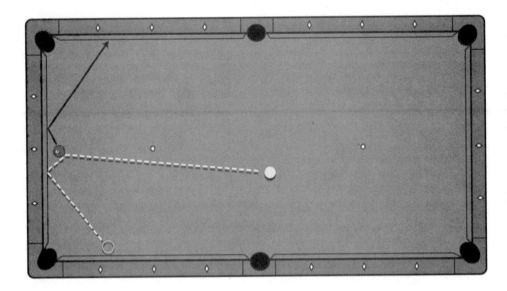

THE END RAIL SAFETY

Here the cue ball is towards the middle of the table and the object ball is just off the end rail cushion at the middle diamond. Too many players try to bank this ball into the corner pocket. This is a low percentage shot even for the professionals. It almost always results in a sell out. The percentage shot is to play a safety leaving both balls against the cushion at about the 1 1/2 side rail diamond location on opposite sides of the table. This is accomplished by applying left english to the cue ball and contacting the object ball with about a half ball hit.

The key to this shot is the speed. Since this is a finesse shot, shorten your bridge and take several warm up strokes at the speed you think will be necessary for the ball placements. If you shoot too softly, your opponent will have a shot at the corner pocket. If you shoot too hard, you will leave a shot into the side or end rail corner pocket. But if you execute correctly, your opponent will be forced to make a difficult bank or a return safety. Practice this shot as this shot comes up quite often. This finesse speed can only be learned with lots of practice.

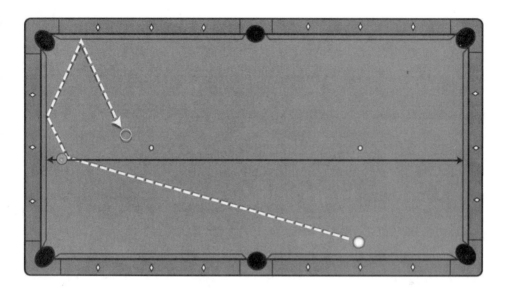

THE LONG END RAIL SAFETY

This shot is very similar to the previous shot except the cue ball is more towards the end of the table and off to the side. While the previous safety could be applied to this shot, the long rail safety is usually a better percentage play. The goal here is to drive the object ball into the cushion and have it rebound straight up the table and have it rest on the end rail cushion. The first key to this shot is striking the proper contact point on the object ball. If the object ball is struck too full, it will rebound from the cushion and contact the cue ball again. This will leave both balls close together. If the object ball is hit too thin, it will travel towards the corner pocket leaving a shot for your opponent.

Always verify the contact point on the object ball by placing the tip of your cue stick underneath the edge of the object ball with the butt end of the stick pointed straight up the table. Now rotate the butt end of the cue stick over the center of the cue ball. This will give you the shooting line to the object ball.

The second key is the execution of the proper speed necessary to get the object ball to the other end of the table. It is normally better to hit this ball a little harder to make sure it contacts the opposite end rail cushion. Since the ball is rolling slowly, much of its energy will be lost after contact with the cushion and it will only roll out a very short distance. Also you are not concerned about the cue ball on this shot. Use a center or slightly above center (like a lag shot) cue ball hit and the cue ball will travel along the rebound tangent line and stay towards the center at the other end of the table.

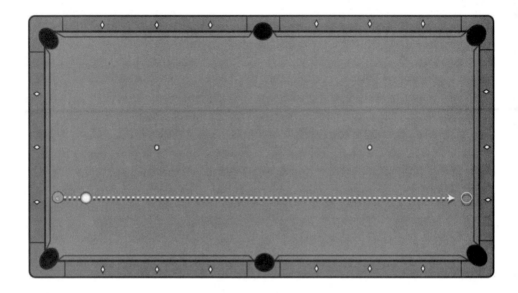

THE SHORT END RAIL SAFETY

The short end rail safety is used when both the cue ball and the object ball are close together, close to the end rail cushion, and aimed straight into the rail. Here you simply shoot the cue ball softly with low english straight into the object ball. The cue ball will stop and the object ball will head towards the cushion. The object ball will then rebound off the cushion sliding right back into the cue ball and virtually stop where it was originally contacted. Now the cue ball will be driven to the other end of the table by the rebounding object ball.

The key to this safety is a slightly below dead center ball hit on the cue ball and a very solid hit on the object ball. If the object ball is struck off center or side spin is applied to the cue ball, the object ball will not rebound off the cushion directly into the cue ball. The rebounding object ball will contact the cue ball towards the side leaving a cut shot for your opponent. You also will note that you do not need much force on this shot to get the rebounding object ball to propel the cue ball to the other end of the table.

This is another finesse shot so use a short bridge and a short loose draw stroke. Cue ball speed is secondary on this shot. While it is great to leave both balls on the cushions at opposite ends of the table, it is more important that your opponent is left with a long bank or a return safety rather than any type of cut shot. Also watch out for a scratch into the corner pocket if the cue ball is stroked too hard and contacted slightly off center. Always play this shot a little short.

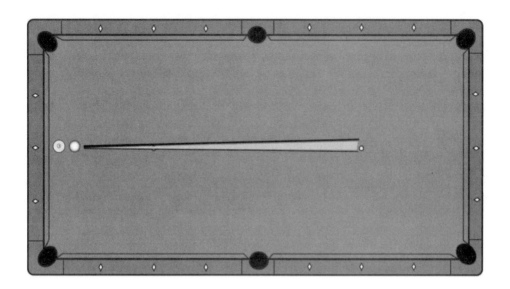

THE TRICKY CLOSE END RAIL SAFETY

I love this safety and have used it many times. Some players have even asked me if it is legal. And of course it is. This set up is very similar to the previous safety, but the balls are closer together and at the middle diamond on the end rail. If you try to just skim the object ball, you have a possible scratch into either corner pocket. If you try to stroke directly into the object ball, you have a possibility of fouling by double hitting the cue ball because both balls are so close together. Also you virtually have to climb up on top of the table to reach this shot or you must use the bridge. None of these are good options.

The way to execute this shot is very simple. Just lay your cue stick on the table and slide the tip under the edge of the cue ball. Be sure the tip does not contact the cue ball. Now grip the cue stick about 3 inches from the tip with your thumb and two fingers. Pull the stick straight up and the tip will contact the edge of the cue ball driving it forward into the object ball. There is no possibility of a double hit on the cue ball with this method. The object ball will then rebound from the rail and strike the cue ball leaving virtually the same shot all over again. This shot requires very little practice and it will dumbfound your opponents if they have never seen it before.

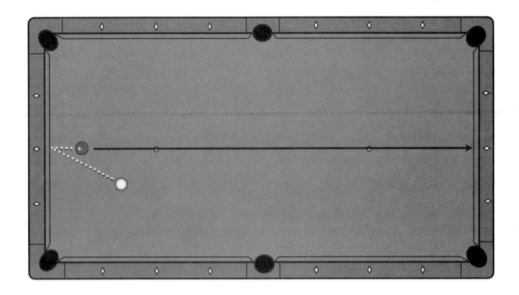

THE END RAIL KICK SAFETY

Sometimes it is better to hit the cushion first with the cue ball before striking the object ball. Your goal here is to stop the cue ball on contact with the object ball and to drive the object ball straight up the table towards the other end. This shot works best when the object ball is only 4-6 inches off the rail and there is about a 25 degree angle from the cue ball to the cushion directly behind the object ball. All you do here is aim to a point on the cushion directly behind the object ball with a little high left english. This will cause the cue ball to rebound straight off the cushion into the object ball, driving it to the other end of the table.

The main key to this shot is to make sure the cue ball is hit with enough force to drive the object ball to the end rail cushion. If it comes up short, you have committed a foul. Second, be sure to strike the object ball as fully as possible. This keeps the object ball away from the corner pockets and the cue ball at the other end of the table close to the rail. This shot is also good to use when the next object ball to be pocketed is by the cue ball. So even if you do leave a shot for your opponents, they must make a very long shot using a rail bridge and get the cue ball all the way back down to the other end of the table for the next shot. This is a good percentage play for you and a bad percentage shot for them.

First practice this shot shooting the cue ball into the end rail cushion with no object ball and see if the opposite english causes the cue ball to go straight up the table into the end rail cushion. This will give you an idea of how much inside english and how much force will be needed to be applied to the cue ball.

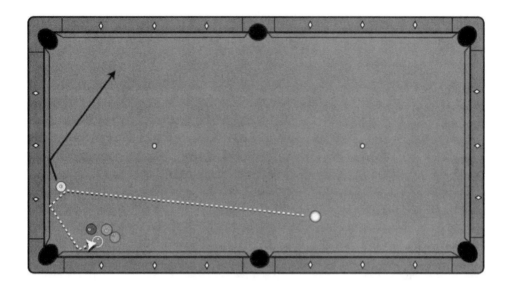

THE DRAW DRAG SAFETY

This is an excellent safety to use when the cue ball is far away from the object ball and you want to keep it close to the end rail after contact with the object ball. Shooting this shot softly and the table conditions can affect the accuracy on this shot. But with the draw drag shot, you strike the cue ball with a little firmer hit and low left english. Aim at the object ball with about a half ball hit. The low english will impart back spin on the cue ball. This back spin on the cue ball will cause more friction against the cloth, causing it to slow as it travels towards the object ball.

As the cue ball approaches the object ball, the backwards spin will dissipate, and the cue ball will begin to roll forward. Now the cue ball will have a slight forward roll and will still have the side spin. Upon contact with the object ball, the cue ball will spin off the object ball into both the end rail and side rail cushions and rebound to behind the cluster of obstructer balls. The object ball will then rebound off the end rail cushion towards the side rail. The draw drag shot is an excellent shot to have in your repertoire. Practice this shot varying the speed, distance, and the amount of low english applied to the cue ball. It will take some practice time before you can acquire the "feel" of this shot in various game situations.

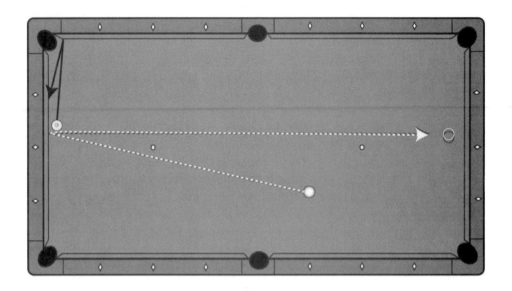

THE END RAIL SHOT/SAFETY PLAY

This is another way to play the end rail shot. This shot comes up quite often in nine ball. Here the object ball is about 1/4 to 3/4 of an inch off the end rail cushion between the first and second diamonds, and the cue ball is at the other end of the table. Now impart high right english on the cue ball and aim at the cushion slightly left of the object ball. The cue ball will spin off the cushion and strike the object ball. There are three positives on this shot:

A slight hit on the object ball will cause it to only move several inches, leaving it against the end rail cushion for your opponent.

A slightly fuller hit will pocket the object ball.

An even more full hit will drive the object ball to the side rail cushion and it will rebound back to the end rail cushion for a good safety.

In all cases, the cue ball will go to the other end of the table. There are two negatives on this shot. If you hit too far away from the object ball, you will miss it entirely, causing a foul and giving up ball-in-hand. Second, the object ball could rattle in the "jaws" of the pocket, leaving your opponent an easy shot. However, the outcome on this shot is usually positive. Also as the object ball moves closer towards the pocket, be careful of the scratch in the corner pocket.

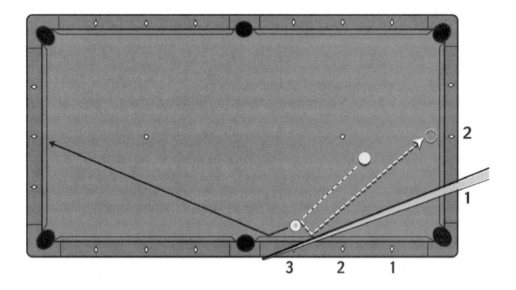

THE SIDE RAIL TO END RAIL SAFETY

Here you virtually do not have a good percentage shot. A bank shot in to the corner pocket or a long rail cut shot are both very low percentage shots. Your goal would be to put the object ball against the end rail cushion at diamond #2 and the cue ball at the other end rail, also at diamond #2. This would leave an extremely difficult bank or a return safety for your opponent. But how do you determine where to hit the object ball to get it to travel to the #2 diamond on the end rail? The next chapter will discuss the various diamond systems in great detail but for this shot, you only need to know that a ball traveling from the #1 diamond on the end rail to the #3 diamond on the side rail will go to the middle diamond on the other end rail. So now just place the cue stick over these two diamonds and parallel shift over to the object ball. The point where the cue stick meets the rail is your contact point for the object ball.

Now place your cue tip about one inch behind the object ball directly inline with the spot on the cushion where you want the object ball to go. Finally, rotate the butt end of the stick over the cue ball while leaving the cue tip behind the object ball. This is the line needed for the cue ball to strike the object ball and drive it to the end rail middle diamond. Apply high left english on the cue ball, and it will also travel back to the opposite end rail middle diamond. Use a finesse stroke so you need to shorten your bridge and take several warm up strokes to obtain the feel needed for the proper speed.

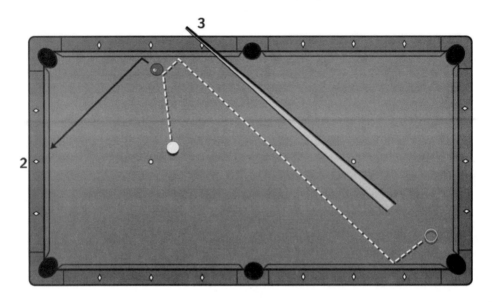

THE OPPOSITE SIDE TO END RAIL SAFETY

This shot is like the previous shot but here the object ball moves a short distance and the cue ball moves much farther. Again, you always start with what you know. A ball hit from the middle diamond on the end rail to the #3 diamond on the side rail will go to the corner pocket. So now you must think a little backwards. If you line up your cue stick from this corner pocket to the #3 diamond on the side rail, this will give us a rebound path off the cushion to the end rail middle diamond. Now parallel shift the cue stick over the object ball.

Like the previous illustration, the spot on the cushion contacted by the cue stick is your object ball contact point. Pull the cue stick back over the top of the object ball and place the tip on the cloth about one inch away directly in line with the side rail cushion contact point. Like before, rotate the butt end of the cue stick over the cue ball leaving the tip on the cloth in front of the object ball. This is the line you must shoot to move the object ball to the end rail middle diamond. Again use a finesse speed stroke with a slightly shorter bridge. Apply right english only to the cue ball. This will cause the cue ball to spin and accelerate off the rail towards the other end of the table. The key is the speed necessary to move the object ball to the middle of the end rail cushion. Anywhere the cue ball ends up at the other end of the table is fine. But be careful of the scratch. Practice this shot using various degrees of right hand english. Always leave the contact point on the object ball the same.

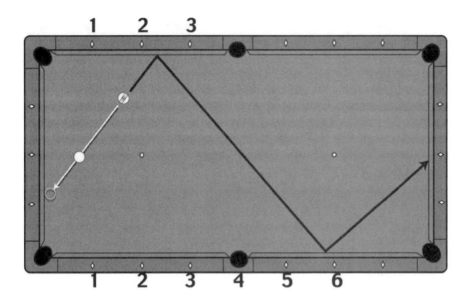

THE TWO RAIL SAFETY

Unfortunately, the above illustration comes up quite often playing 9 ball. It usually results from allowing the cue ball to travel too far down from the other end of the table after pocketing the 8 ball. Now you are left with a difficult bank on the 9 ball into the side pocket. A miss usually results in a lost game. The percentage play is to play a safety, banking the 9 ball two rails to the middle diamond on the far end rail cushion while drawing the cue ball back to the opposite end rail cushion.

To get a feel for this shot, first place an object ball in the "jaws" of the corner pocket closest to the cue ball. Shoot this object ball with a slightly above dead center hit across the table into the #3 diamond, and it will rebound to diamond #6 on the opposite side rail (angle in equals angle out). The object ball will then rebound off the side cushion to the middle diamond on the end rail cushion. Repeatedly shoot this shot until you can consistently get the object ball to stop close to the end rail cushion at the middle diamond. You have now obtained the "feel" for the speed needed for this shot.

Now go to the actual set up shot. Shoot the shot with draw english so the cue ball will back up to the opposite end rail. Do not use the donuts on this shot. Vary it slightly each time. This will show you how the contact point on the cushion moves slightly up or down at diamond #3 in order to obtain the desired object ball location at the end rail middle diamond.

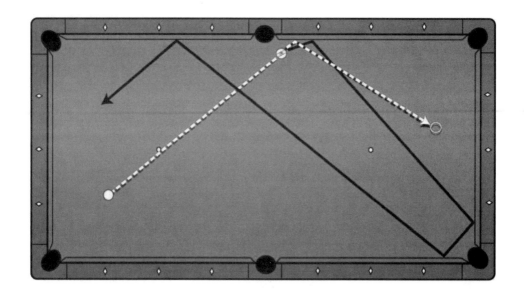

THE FOUR RAIL SAFETY

Professional pool and billiard instructor, Wayne Norcross, loves this safety. Usually this shot occurs when your opponents have played bad position on the nine ball and they try to cut it or bank it into the side pocket. They have strategically left the 9 ball slightly above the side pocket. You cannot cut the 9 ball into the side pocket and shooting it into the corner pocket would result in a cue ball scratch in the side pocket. The percentage shot here is to play safe, shooting the nine ball into the side rail. Use a firm stroke and just a little high english on the cue ball. The nine ball will go four rails and end up on the end rail cushion at about the middle diamond. The cue ball will follow forward into the side rail cushion and drift down to the end rail cushion also at diamond #2. This will leave a very difficult shot for your opponent. The key to this shot is to be sure the nine ball is hit with enough force to drive it to the end rail cushion. Leaving it short will leave a shot for your opponent.

Any time your cue ball is positioned below the nine ball (as in the previous Two Rail Safety illustration) and you decide to shoot it into the side pocket, aim one of the following two ways. If you are cutting it into the side pocket, aim to the bottom side of the pocket. A miss to this side will leave the nine ball above the side pocket. Hitting the opposite side pocket corner will leave the nine ball in front of the side pocket. If you bank the nine ball, aim a little long. A miss here will leave the nine ball above the side pocket. A miss on the short side will leave the nine ball in front of the side pocket.

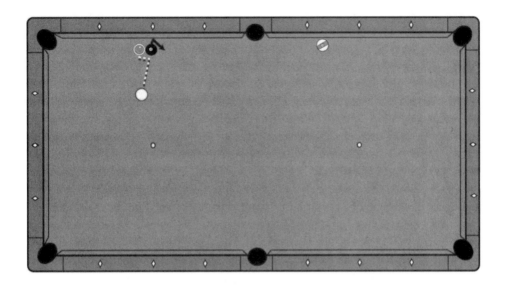

THE SIMPLEST EIGHT BALL SAFETY

Eight ball is as much a strategy game as it is a position game. Since most 8 ball tournaments are played on the smaller tables, many innings are ended by being hooked or
blocked on a shot rather than missing a shot. Most of the better players will analyze the
table. Then they will run several balls and play safety so their opponents must kick at
their ball. The key to these safeties is to get the cue ball as close to your object ball as
possible. This will cut off many of the kicking routes discussed in the next chapter. The
less kicking options your opponents have will greatly reduce their ability to make a
legal hit on their balls.

Set the shot up as illustrated above. The goal here is to slowly contact the solid ball
slightly off center with the cue ball. The solid ball will then rebound slightly off the cushion and the cue ball will drift forward to about where the object ball was. This will leave
both balls very close together with the solid ball blocking the path to the striped ball.
This is a finesse speed shot so use a short bridge and backstroke. Be sure to take several warm up strokes at the speed you think is necessary to accomplish the proper position of the balls. Many players make the fatal mistake of not taking these warm up
strokes to obtain the proper feel for this shot. That is the #1 reason these safeties are not
executed properly.

Chapter Four
The Kicking Game

Giving up ball-in-hand is the worst thing you can do in the game of nine ball. This chapter is the largest in the book and discusses very easy to learn 1, 2, 3, & 4 rail kicking systems. None of these systems requires a calculator or higher math skills to figure out. I call this the "WORLD OF PARALLELS". You basically learn or memorize these basic connect-the-diamonds systems. Then when you are in a game situation, take the system you know that will hit the obstructed object ball and "parallel shift" over to the cue ball. It really is that simple.

But before you can learn these systems, you must understand a little more about the table. All tables are perfect rectangles with the length twice the width. What you are most concerned about is the actual playing surface. For an example, on a 9 foot table the width of the table cushion to cushion is 50 inches and the length is 100 inches. The balls are 2 1/4 inches in diameter and most cue sticks are about 58 inches long. The distance between the diamonds is exactly 12 1/2 inches. Ninety nine percent of all pool players do not know this number but it is very easy to calculate - 50" width divided by 4 diamonds equals 12 1/2", or 100" length divided by 8 diamonds equals 12 1/2". Also most standard pockets are about 4 & 5/8 inches wide with the side pocket about 1 inch larger. Do not overlook these side pockets as they are "buckets" with an error margin of about 2 1/2 balls. It is important to know these numbers and how they relate to each other on a given shot.

Also for the purpose of this chapter, you must not think of the table as a rectangle but more like a group of triangles (Fig. #1). Virtually everything you do in pool involves angles. Generally speaking, when a ball goes into a rail cushion at an angle, it will release from the rail cushion at the same opposite angle. There are many factors that can influence this release angle. The following are some of the factors:

SPEED - More compression of the cushion occurs with a higher speed resulting in a narrower release angle.

ENGLISH - Spin will shorten or widen the release angle.

HUMIDITY - Alters cushions/cloth and affects "cling".

CLEANLINESS OF CLOTH/BALLS - Affects slide & roll.

So put your thinking cap on and proceed to the various systems. You must be able to memorize, visualize, and understand each of these simple systems. You now will begin giving up ball-in-hand much less and even making balls you were unable to hit before. Welcome to the "WORLD OF PARALLELS."

For illustration purposes in this chapter, I will not clutter up the table diagrams with blocker or obstructer balls. You will assume that the direct route or other kicking routes to the object ball are blocked. Second, most illustrated kicks will have an object ball in front of a pocket. This accomplishes two things. First, it gives immediate positive feedback when the kick is executed correctly. Second, it will give you a visualization and memorization of the various track lines the cue ball travels as it rebounds off the cushion(s). As these track lines are learned, you will be able to hit or even make the object ball any where along the track line. Once you have become proficient at making the object ball in front of the pocket, experiment by moving the object ball away from the pocket along the track line. If you make or contact the object ball fairly fully, then you have visualized the track line correctly.

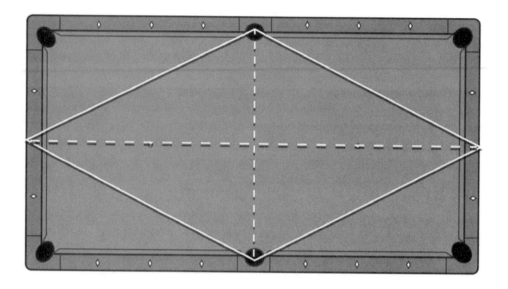

THE TRIANGLE (Fig. #1)

Since the table is a rectangle, the middle diamonds of each rail connect to make a group of triangles. For the purposes of this chapter, you must begin to think of the table as a whole bunch of different angles and triangles. By looking at the illustration above, you have already learned several kicking shots. If you have an object ball at the end rail middle diamond and the cue ball at the other end rail middle diamond, you just have to aim at either side rail middle diamond to kick at the ball. Or if the cue ball is in front of the side pocket and the object ball is in front of the other side pocket, you just aim at the middle diamond on the end rail to kick the object ball into the pocket. If the cue ball is at the end rail middle diamond and the object ball is in front of the side pocket, you just aim at the other side rail middle diamond and the cue ball will travel two rails and contact the object ball.

So now you have already learned one track line that can be used for several shots. The table is comprised of an infinite amount of track lines. The goal for this chapter is to teach only some of these track lines. Once you have learned and memorized these, you can use your knowledge of the "parallel shift" and virtually kick at any ball.

ONE RAIL KICKING

One rail kicking is the easiest as it usually involves simple division math. In almost all one rail kicks, you should use a medium stroke with a dead center or slightly above center (running english) hit. A good stroke with an accurate cue ball hit is imperative for all kicking shots. This is because most kicks require the cue ball to travel a farther distance than normal before contacting the object ball. Accuracy is always eroded when the cue ball travels farther.

Study, memorize, and practice the following kicking systems. You will be amazed at how easy they are to learn and execute. I guarantee your opponents will get a lot less chances with "ball-in-hand". You are now just beginning to enter the "WORLD OF PARALLELS". Enjoy your newly found skills.

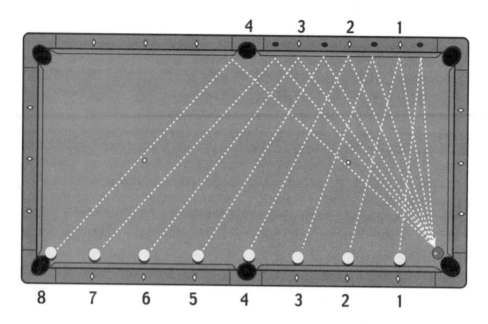

SIMPLE DIVISION KICKING

This is probably the easiest system to use. Number each of the diamonds on the side rails 1 through 8. Since you know the table is a perfect rectangle and the cue ball is located at diamond #8, you just divide this number by 2 and aim at the #4 diamond on the opposite rail to make the object ball in front of the corner pocket. The #4 diamond is the halfway point between the cue ball and the object ball. If the cue ball is at diamond #3, you simply aim at the 1 1/2 diamond mark on the side rail. Memorize these "tracks" and you will be able to kick one rail at any ball. If the cue ball is not exactly at a diamond, just parallel shift over with your cue stick from the closest known track to the cue ball. This will give you the new contact point on the side rail cushion. This shot should be shot with a medium stroke and dead center or slightly above dead center ball hit. Any side english imparted on the cue ball will vary the rebound angle off the cushion.

Practice this shot starting with the cue ball close to the side rail cushion at diamond #1 moving up the rail to diamond #8. Within a short amount of practice time, you should be able to make the corner object ball from all eight positions. After you have become proficient at these locations, place the cue ball arbitrarily along the side rail cushion. Find the closest known track line and "parallel shift" the cue stick over to the cue ball to give you the new contact point on the opposite cushion. It is really that simple.

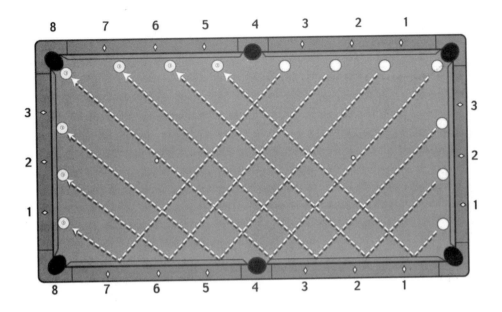

THE CORNER ONE RAIL KICK

The above diamond systems and tracks need to be memorized. At first glance, this illustration looks very complicated. But in essence it is very simple. First start with what you already know. You know if you shoot the cue ball out of the upper right corner pocket at the side rail #4 diamond, the cue ball will rebound off the cushion towards the object ball in front of the pocket at the #8 diamond. Now notice if you move one diamond to either side of this track and remain parallel to this line, the cue ball will rebound off the cushion and travel one diamond to the left or right of the corner pocket. If you move two diamonds away from your original corner pocket track and remain parallel, the cue ball will rebound off the cushion two diamonds away from the object ball in front of the corner pocket.

Notice how these track lines remain virtually parallel to each other. So even though I have numbered the diamonds, it is not necessary to memorize the number tracks. It is fine to know that going from the #2 diamond on the side rail to the #6 diamond on the other side rail will result in the cue ball continuing to the #2 diamond on the end rail. It is just easier to remember that if you parallel shift two diamonds away from the corner pocket track, the cue ball will move two diamonds away from the other corner pocket. Practice shooting the above seven shots. Once you are able to hit the object ball at each location consistently, place the cue ball away from these track lines and practice parallel shifting from the closest known track line.

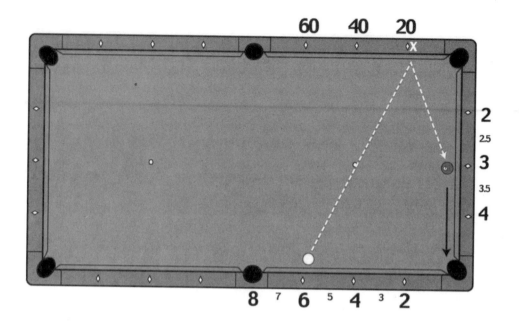

THE HALF TABLE END RAIL KICKING SYSTEM

This is the best system to use when both the cue ball and the object ball are on the same end of the table with the object ball close to the end rail cushion and the cue ball is close to the side rail cushion. First, assign the numbers 2, 3, & 4 to the end rail diamonds as illustrated. Next, assign the numbers 2, 4, 6, & 8 to the cue ball side rail diamonds. And finally, the far side rail diamonds are assigned the numbers 20, 40, & 60. Now it becomes a simple multiplication problem. In the above illustration, the cue ball is located at diamond #6 on the side rail. The object ball is located at diamond #3 on the end rail. Now just multiply these two numbers (3 X 6 =18). You have calculated the number 18 as the one you want to hit with the cue ball on the opposite side rail. Now find diamond #20 and move the contact point slightly down towards the pocket. Hit the cue ball with a soft to medium stroke and a dead center ball hit. Any english imparted on the cue ball will affect the rebound angle.

Practice this shot until you can consistently make the object ball or drive it close to the pocket. Then vary the position of the cue ball and practice your multiplication skills. Finally, vary the position of the object ball. Remember your point of calculation for the object ball is the point of contact and not the center of the object ball.

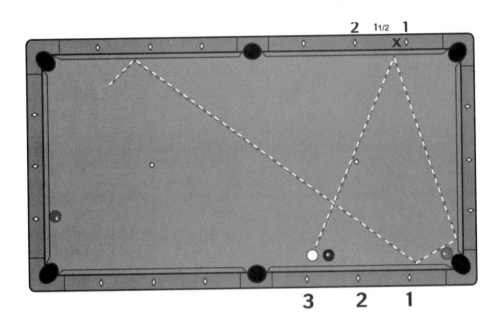

THE ONE RAIL POSITION KICK

In the above illustration, you are not only blocked to your object ball, but you must get to the other end of the table for your next shot. Since your cue ball is at diamond #3 on the side rail, your contact point on the opposite side rail is the 1 1/2 diamond mark (3 divided by 2 equals 1 1/2). This will give you a full hit on the object ball and leave the cue ball in front of the pocket with no shot on the next object ball. What you need to do is have the cue ball strike the end cushion first before it contacts the object ball. The cue ball will then carom off the object ball towards the other end of the table. You simply accomplish this by moving your contact point on the cushion about 1/4 diamond down the rail from your original calculation. This will widen the angle the cue ball rebounds from the cushion, and it will contact the end rail cushion just before the object ball. Be careful not to add too much speed. The increased speed of the cue ball will compress the cushion more and shorten the angle. On dirty or slow tables, you may need to move the contact point down slightly more to compensate for the increased speed and the lesser rebound angle.

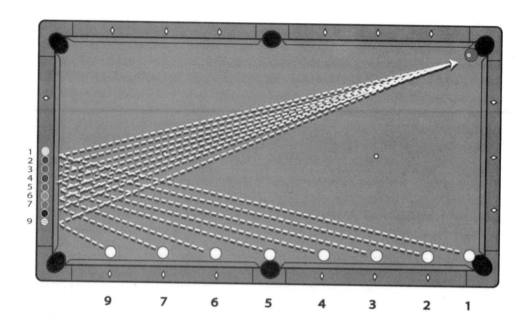

LONG RAIL VISUALIZATION KICKING

Long rail kicking is more difficult because the cue ball usually has to travel a longer distance, increasing the margin for error. Learn and memorize the above tracks. As before, start with the cue ball in front of the corner pocket. By aiming at the middle diamond on the end rail, the cue ball will rebound off the cushion towards the object ball in front of the opposite corner pocket. Now imagine a string of nine balls on the end rail, beginning at the middle diamond and proceeding towards the pocket. As the cue ball moves up the long rail one diamond, the contact point on the cushion moves over 1 ball.

As it moves to the second diamond, the cushion contact point moves another ball. This system continues to work as you go up the rail until you get to the last diamond. At this point, the contact on the end rail cushion moves over one additional (2 balls from the previous diamond) ball. Again, notice how all these tracks run parallel to your original known track. When kicking from the 2-4 spots, your calculated contact point should be verified by parallel shifting over to the known corner to end rail middle diamond track line. When kicking from the 5-9 spots, verify your contact point with the known #1 end rail diamond to the third side rail diamond track. Use a soft to medium stroke with about 1/2 tip of high english only.

A great way to practice this system is to actually place the one through nine balls on the rail as illustrated with the numbers facing forward. The easiest way to do this is to place a chalk directly on the middle end diamond and place the one ball on top of the chalk. Now place another chalk next to the one ball and place the two ball on top of this chalk frozen to the one ball. Continue placing each ball on top of a chalk and frozen to the previous ball until all nine balls are in a line on the end rail. Now simply aim directly at the numbered ball that corresponds with the side rail diamond number. With very little practice, you should be able to pocket the opposite corner object ball almost every time from any of these positions.

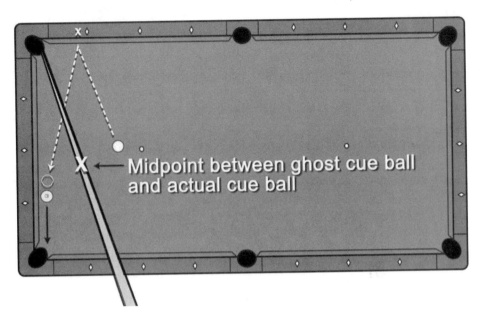

Midpoint between ghost cue ball and actual cue ball

THE MIDPOINT KICKING SYSTEM (SIDE RAIL)

This system works best when the cue ball is more towards the center of the table and there is not a lot of distance between the object ball and the cue ball. The first thing you must do is visualize the cue ball (ghost ball) lined up against the object ball aimed directly into the corner pocket. This determines the point of contact where the cue ball must strike the object ball to make it into the corner pocket. Next, you take the cue stick and place the cue tip in the middle of the opposite corner pocket while keeping the stick equal distance between the "ghost cue ball" and the actual cue ball. This will determine the midpoint between the two balls. Now parallel shift the cue stick over to the cue ball. The spot on the rail cushion contacted by the cue stick is the point the cue ball must contact to make the object ball.

The key to this kicking system is to always calculate the midpoint between the "ghost cue ball" and the actual cue ball. I have seen many players use this system incorrectly by determining the midpoint between the object ball and cue ball. Use a soft to medium stroke with a dead center or slightly above center hit on the cue ball.

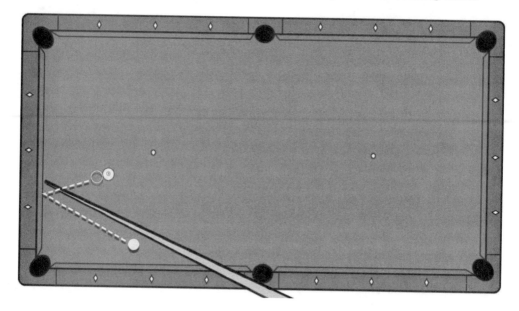

THE MIDPOINT KICKING SYSTEM (END RAIL)

The above illustration uses a similar principle as the previous example but the object ball is not close to a pocket. Again, imagine a "ghost cue ball" lined up against the object ball to make it into the far corner pocket. Now place your cue tip on the cushion directly behind this ghost ball. Rotate the butt end of the stick until it is halfway between the "ghost cue ball" and the actual cue ball. Now simply parallel shift over to the cue ball and the point where the cue stick contacts the cushion is the rebound contact point to make the object ball into the corner pocket. Use a center ball hit on the cue ball or slightly above center hit to hold the cue ball close to the rail after contact with the object ball.

This shot is an excellent two way shot especially when the next ball to be pocketed is also close to the end rail by the object ball. If the object ball is missed, it is usually left close to the far end rail. Now your opponents have a difficult long shot off the rail and must come all the way back to the other end of the table for their next shot. The two key factors on this shot are to calculate the contact point on the cushion properly and to make sure you hit it hard enough for the object ball to contact the cushion if it is not made. Remember, you are hitting the cushion first on this shot so some of the speed will be taken off the cue ball as it rebounds off the cushion. You do not want to give up ball-in-hand by committing a foul on this shot by failing to have the object ball contact the end rail cushion.

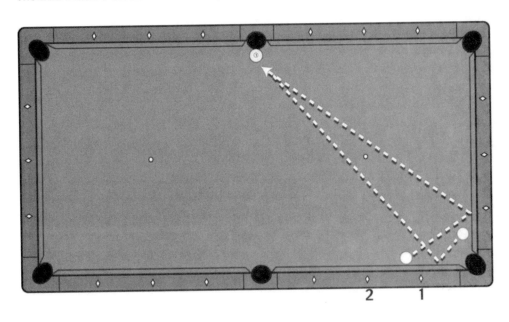

ONE RAIL SIDE POCKET KICKS

The above two illustrated kicks are simply connect-the-diamond shots. On the first shot, the cue ball is close to the end rail cushion and directly in line with the two corner diamonds. By aiming into the side rail diamond #1 and using a firm stroke with a center ball hit on the cue ball, the cue ball will rebound off the side rail cushion towards the side pocket. This 1 to 1 track line is virtually a 40 degree angle in resulting with a rebound angle of 40 degrees out.

The second shot has the cue ball close to the side rail cushion. It is directly in line with the side rail #2 diamond and the end rail #1 diamond. Here you simply stroke the cue ball with a little running english (high left) into the end rail #1 diamond, and the cue ball will pocket the object ball in front of the side pocket. Be careful not to shoot this shot too hard as the cue ball can carom off the object ball for a scratch into the corner pocket. This is a simple 2 to 1 track line.

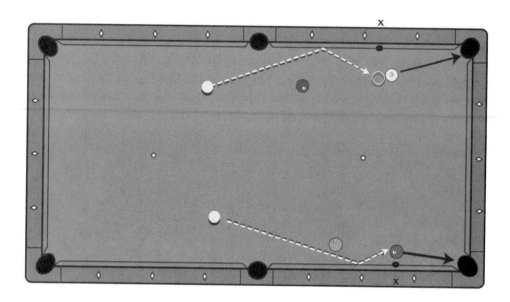

EQUAL DISTANCE KICKING

Many times you are left with what would normally be a nice easy shot close to the rail and pocket, but you have a blocker ball between the cue ball and the object ball. These kick shots are much easier than you think. In the bottom example, the edge of the object ball is less than 2 inches from the cushion. Now measure the distance from the center of the object ball to the cushion. Next take this same distance from the edge of the cushion into the rail. Place your finger on this spot and extend the cue stick from this spot to the cue ball. You now have two reference points to shoot at. You can either aim at the spot on the rail or the spot on the cushion where your cue stick crosses from the rail spot to the cue ball. Most players prefer to aim at the rail spot. Shoot this shot softly with a dead center ball hit.

In the top example, the edge of the object ball is 2-4 inches from the rail. Place an imaginary ghost cue ball directly in front of the object ball, aimed directly into the pocket. Now measure the distance from the center of the imaginary ghost ball to the cushion. Take this same distance again from the edge of the cushion into the rail. You have now determined the spot on the rail that will give you the shooting line into the cushion to pocket the ball. Basically what this means is as your object ball moves away from the rail, your point of contact moves farther up the cushion. Again shoot softly with a center ball hit. I do not suggest you try to make balls farther than 4-5 inches from the cushion because usually the object ball fails to be contacted resulting in a foul.

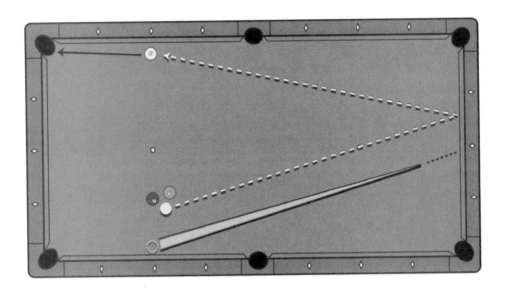

THE MIDDLE DIAMOND GHOST CUE BALL KICKING SYSTEM - LONG RAIL

While I have left this one rail kicking system at the end of this section, it is probably the easiest to learn. Professional pool and billiard instructor, Calvin Coker, has been teaching this system to his students for years. What makes this system so easy is that your starting reference point is always the middle diamond on the end rail. Note the above diagram where the intended object ball is blocked by two obstructer balls. The first thing to do is to determine the exact location of the object ball that must be hit. Now place your finger on the cloth on the opposite side of the table where this object ball would be located if it were a mirror image of the actual ball. Now both the actual object ball and the mirror image object ball (ghost cue ball) are exactly the same distances from both the side and end rail cushions but on opposite sides of the table. So if you were to shoot from this location to the end rail middle diamond with a slightly above dead center cue ball hit, the ghost cue ball would rebound off the cushion towards the object ball on the opposite side of the table. But since your actual cue ball is not at this location, you simply create a line to the end rail middle diamond spot from the ghost cue ball position with the cue stick. Now finally parallel shift the cue stick over to the actual cue ball, and the cue tip will point at your new contact point on the end rail cushion to kick at the intended object ball. It is really that simple!

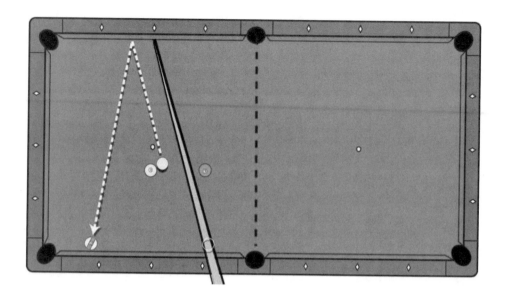

THE MIDDLE DIAMOND GHOST CUE BALL KICKING SYSTEM - SHORT RAIL

The only difference between this diagram and the previous page is that here you are shooting into the side rail cushion versus the end rail cushion. Since both the object ball and cue ball are on the same side of the table, simply divide the table in half (dotted line to the side pockets). You now have created two perfect squares but are only concerned with the one containing the balls. Now the reference point on the side rail is always the middle diamond (the diamond half way between the side pocket and corner pocket). Again, determine the mirror image of the object ball on the other side of the square. In this case, the object ball is about 1 1/4 diamonds down from the side rail middle diamond and slightly off the cushion. So the ghost cue ball position is 1 1/4 diamonds to the other side of the middle diamond and also slightly off the cushion. Repeat the alignment procedure as before. Place the cue stick over the center of the ghost cue ball position and aim the cue tip at the middle diamond on the opposite rail. Parallel shift the cue stick from this line over the cue ball, and the cue tip again will point at your new contact point on the side rail cushion.

By now, you have probably figured out you can use this system anywhere on the table. If you can equally separate the object ball from the ghost cue ball position equal distance from a spot on the opposite rail, you can always parallel shift to the cue ball and determine the actual kicking line. What do you think of this " WORLD OF PARALLELS" now!

ENGLISH KICKING

There are many times when the normal kicking path to the object ball is blocked. This is when you must create your own angle by using english on the cue ball. By applying english to the cue ball in the direction the cue ball is traveling (running english), you will widen or lengthen the angle the cue ball rebounds from the rail. Conversely, if you apply english to the cue ball opposite to its direction of travel (holding english), the rebound angle of the cue ball off the rail will shorten or narrow. You will be surprised how often these situations come up when your normal angle is blocked. Practice and memorize the following examples. Soon you will get a feel of how much english to apply to get the desired results.

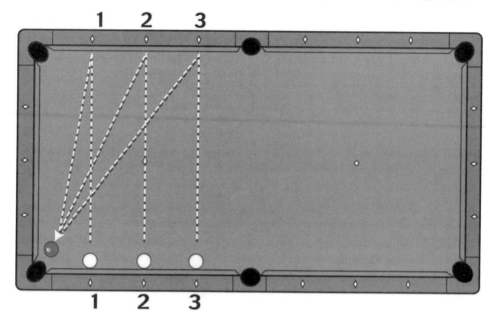

SIDE RAIL ENGLISH KICKS

Sometimes obstructer balls block the normal kicking angle path to the object ball. In these situations, these obstructer balls force a change in the contact point on the cushion. This would cause the cue ball to not contact the object ball using a center ball hit. By adding english to the cue ball you can change the release angle of the cue ball from the cushion.

The above illustration shows how the use of various degrees of english applied to the cue ball can kick the object ball into the corner pocket from different positions. When the cue ball is along the side rail cushion at diamond #1, aim straight across the table at diamond #1 with high left english (11 o'clock) and the cue ball will rebound off the cushion towards the object ball in front of the corner pocket. When the cue ball is at diamond #2, again aim straight across the table at diamond #2 using only left english (9 o'clock), and the cue ball will rebound off the cushion at a wider angle towards the corner pocket. And finally as the cue ball moves up to diamond #3, again shoot straight across the table at diamond #3 with low left english (7 o'clock). The cue ball will now rebound off the cushion at a much wider angle towards the corner pocket.

This side rail system can be used anywhere on the table. By using various degrees of english and shooting softly straight across the table, you can move the cue ball 1, 2, or 3 diamonds. The greater the rebound angle needed, the slower the cue ball must be hit.

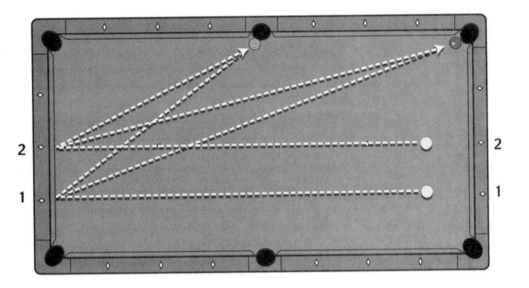

END RAIL ENGLISH KICKS

End rail english kicking is more difficult than side rail kicking as more distance is involved. Here again the normal path to kick the object ball into the corner pocket is blocked. At diamond position #1, aim straight up the table at diamond #1 applying right english on the cue ball with a very firm stroke. The cue ball will then rebound off the cushion towards the corner pocket. At diamond #2, use high right english and take a little speed off the shot using a moderate to firm stroke. Again, the cue ball will rebound off the end cushion at a lesser angle towards the corner pocket.

An object ball can also be kicked into the side pocket from these same positions. At diamond position #1, aim straight at diamond #1 on the far end rail but shoot the cue ball softly with right english only. The cue ball will rebound off the end rail cushion at a more severe angle than before, towards the side pocket. At diamond position #2, again aim straight up the table at the end rail diamond #2 but shoot softly with high right english. This shot requires a little more right english (about at 2 oclock) than the corner kick shot. Once you obtain a degree of consistency on these illustrations, vary the cue ball placement. You can kick either of these two balls into the pocket from virtually anywhere on the table by shooting straight into the end rail cushion and varying the speed and the amount on spin applied to the cue ball. Soon you will develop a "feel" for the predictable cushion release angles.

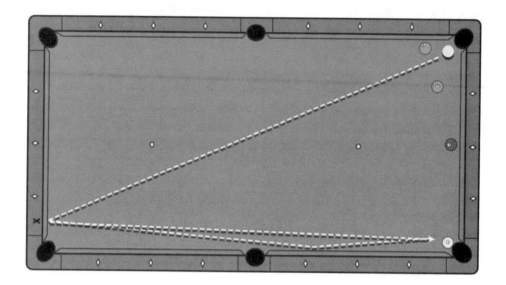

OPPOSITE ENGLISH HOLD KICKING

Opposite english (spin in the opposite direction the cue ball is traveling) kicking is more difficult and less predictable than running english kicking. In the above illustration, the cue ball is in front of one corner pocket and the object ball is in front of the opposite corner pocket with virtually all normal kicking paths blocked. By aiming at about the 1/2 diamond mark on the end rail cushion with a very firm stroke and extreme (about 1 1/2 tips) right english, the cue ball will rebound off the end rail cushion almost straight down the table towards the object ball. The margin for error is quite large on this shot because the cue ball can rebound off the end rail cushion towards the first diamond up on the side rail and still make the object ball into the corner pocket. So the margin for error to make the object ball is about eight inches between the edge of the object ball and the first diamond on the side rail cushion.

A very firm stroke is needed for this shot for two reasons. Number one is that the maximum amount of side spin on the cue ball when it contacts the end cushion is needed after it has traveled the length of the table. Number two is that the end cushion needs to be compressed as much as possible to aid in lessening the rebound angle. Again, these are last resort shots. Practice these also by varying the cue ball position, end rail contact point (remember parallel shift), and the amount of english applied to the cue ball.

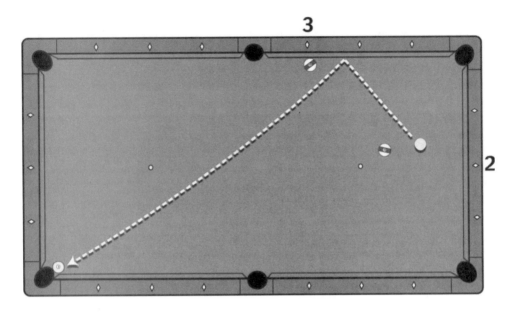

THE HIGH ENGLISH LOOP KICK SHOT

In the above illustration, your known path (end rail #2 diamond to the side rail #3 diamond) to kick the object ball into the corner pocket is blocked by other obstructer balls. These obstructer balls force you to parallel shift back from your known line to a point on the cushion away from the obstructer ball. This new line will cause the cue ball to rebound off the cushion at a narrower angle towards the opposite side rail away from the object ball in front of the corner pocket. You need to figure out a way the cue ball path can be altered towards the object ball after it rebounds off the cushion past the obstructer ball. This can be accomplished by using a very firm stroke and about 1 1/2 cue tips of high english (top spin). The cue ball will first rebound off the cushion at a straight angle for about one foot as it slides. Then the cue ball will begin to roll forward and the high english spin will cause the cue ball to grip the cloth and bend or "loop" the cue ball towards the end rail object ball in front of the corner pocket.

Spend some time practicing this shot. Set this shot up using the white reinforcement donuts. Now vary both the speed and the amount of high english used. Notice how both of these can alter the amount of bend on the cue ball. Proper execution in game situations on these type of shots can be crowd-pleasers and opponent-demoralizers.

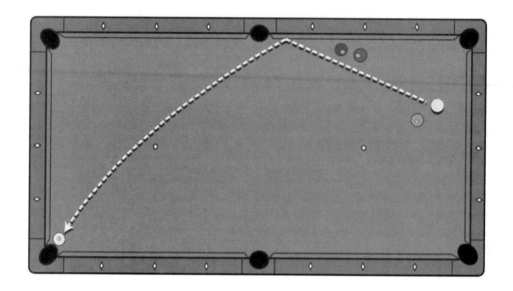

THE DRAW ENGLISH HOLD KICK SHOT

This shot is very similar to the loop kick shot. Again your normal 2 to 3 line to the corner pocket is blocked. This time you are forced to move your contact point farther up the rail towards the side pocket. This new line will cause the cue ball to rebound off the cushion at a wider angle towards the end rail away from the object ball in front of the corner pocket. You must figure out a way to bend or "hold" the cue ball back towards the object ball. This is accomplished with a medium to firm stroke and about 1 1/2 cue tips of low english (reverse spin). After the cue ball rebounds off the cushion, the low english spin will cause the cue ball to grip the cloth and draw back away from its natural line towards the object ball in front of the corner pocket.

Again, practice this shot using the donuts for a consistent set up. Then vary the speed and amount of low english used. Notice again how this bending of the cue ball can be altered. You should now have a feel of how the cue ball path can be altered after rebounding off the cushion by using either high or low english with varying speeds.

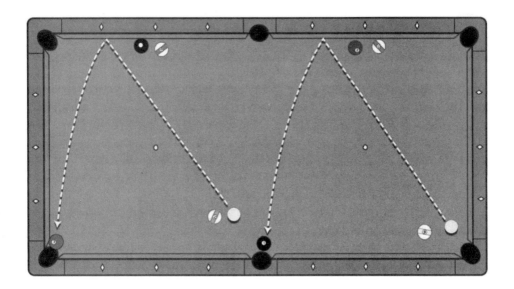

THE EXTREME HOLD KICK SHOT

The above illustration shows two more examples of the hold kick shot. In the one on the left, the known side pocket to the second side rail diamond path is blocked to kick the object ball into the corner pocket. By moving the cushion contact point one diamond towards the corner pocket and applying low right english to the cue ball with a firm stroke, the cue ball will be released from the cushion at a narrower angle and bend towards the object ball. The reverse spin on the cue ball narrows the release angle off the cushion and the draw english bends the cue ball towards the object ball.

The shot on the right is very similar to the shot on the left. Here the known kicking path from the corner pocket to the second diamond on side rail to the side pocket is blocked. By moving the cushion contact point one diamond up towards the side pocket and applying low right english with a firm stroke, the cue ball will rebound off the rail and bend towards the object ball in front of the side pocket. Again the reverse english on the cue ball narrows the release angle off the cushion, and the bottom spin on the cue ball will bend the cue ball towards the object ball as it proceeds along the cloth.

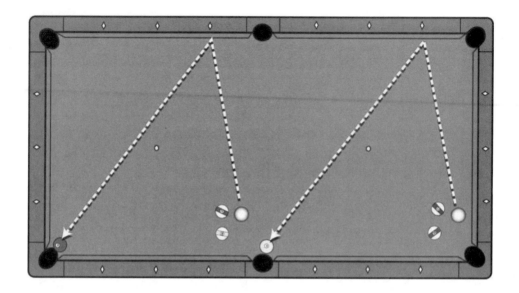

SIDE RAIL ENGLISH KICKING

The above illustration is a duplicate of the previous page but shows another way to kick at the same balls. On the one on the left, the normal kicking path and the "hold" kicking path are both blocked. Here you move the contact point one diamond back from your known second diamond path. By shooting softly and applying left english to the cue ball, the cue ball will spin off the side rail cushion at a wider angle towards the corner object ball in front of the corner pocket.

Again, the shot on the right is similar to the shot on the left. Both the known kicking path and the hold kicking path are blocked. By moving the cushion contact point one diamond back from the normal known path to the first diamond and applying left english to the cue ball with a soft stroke, the cue ball will rebound off the side rail cushion at a wider angle towards the object ball in front of the side pocket.

By now, you should really be getting a feel for how the cue ball rebounds off the cushion at a fairly predictable angle with various degrees of english and speed. Your confidence at hitting and making the "blocked" object ball should be building with this newly acquired knowledge.

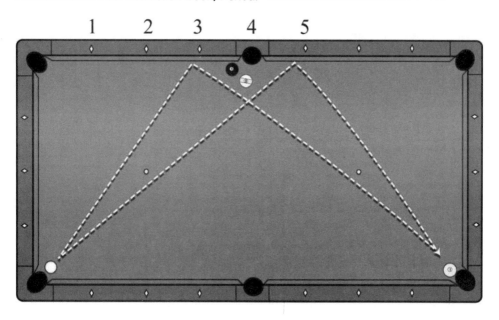

VARIATIONS OF THE CORNER ONE RAIL KICK

You learned in the one rail kicking section that the cue ball coming out of the corner pocket into the side rail cushion at the #4 diamond pockets the object ball in the opposite corner pocket. In the above illustration your normal path is blocked. But now you have learned that by adjusting your cushion contact point one diamond either way and applying the appropriate english to the cue ball, the cue ball will arrive at the same desired location. If you adjust your contact point back to diamond #3, you simply apply right english to the cue ball to widen the angle with a soft to moderate stroke.

If you shift your contact point down the cushion to diamond #5, you use a moderate to firm stroke applying low english on the cue ball. The firm hit narrows the cue ball angle, and the low spin works against the forward momentum of the cue ball on the cloth to bring the cue ball back towards the object ball in front of the corner pocket.

By now you should realize that any time the cue ball is forced to deviate from its normal path to a desired location, the following three things should be determined before you shoot:

1) Speed of the cue ball (soft, medium, or hard hit)

2) Type of english applied (high, low, side, or combination)

3) Amount of english applied (1/4 to 1 1/2 tips away from center)

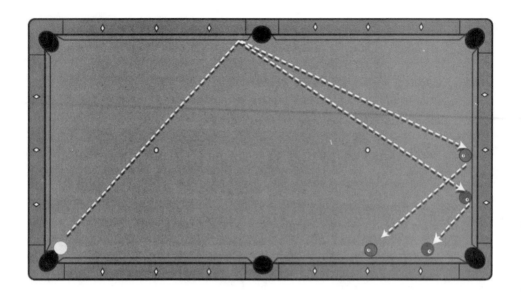

KICKING AWAY FROM THE CORNER POCKET

In most cases, the ball that you will have to kick at is not in the "jaws" of the pocket as most of the illustrations show. But in all learning, there has to be a starting point. Once you have learned the "tracks" and know the theory on how to deviate from these tracks to have the cue ball arrive at its intended destination, you will virtually be able to hit any ball on the table.

In the above illustration, the object ball to be hit is either on the end rail cushion or the side rail cushion. Again you take what you know. The cue ball hit slowly with 1/2 tip of high english coming out of the corner pocket to the middle diamond on the side rail pockets the opposite corner object ball. If you want to hit the object ball at either the first diamond on the end rail cushion or side rail cushion, you aim at the normal spot on the cushion at the middle side rail diamond with a medium stroke and apply high right (running) english on the cue ball. The right english widens the rebound angle off the cushion away from the pocket towards the object ball.

If you want to hit the object ball at the second diamond on the end rail or side rail, you aim at the same spot using a slower speed and low right english. The cue ball will come off the side rail cushion at an even wider angle and strike the object ball at the second diamond on the end rail cushion or continue on to the second diamond on the side rail cushion. So two rail kicking is only a continuation of one rail kicking. This leads you into the two rail kicking part of this chapter.

TWO RAIL KICKING

Kicking two rails is a little more difficult than one rail kicking. Most require a little more knowledge and memorization of the diamond system. Almost all require a running english (a little high and side) hit on the cue ball. Practice each of these exercises. As you become more proficient at each of these illustrations, you will learn the "tracks" or path the cue ball travels. This will enable you to kick at and hit any object ball at any position along this track. Then in a game situation, find the track to the object ball that you know and just parallel shift over to the cue ball.

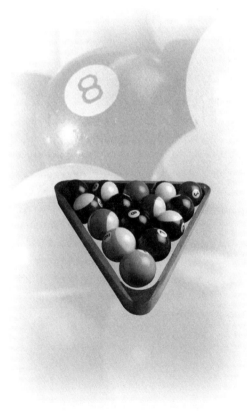

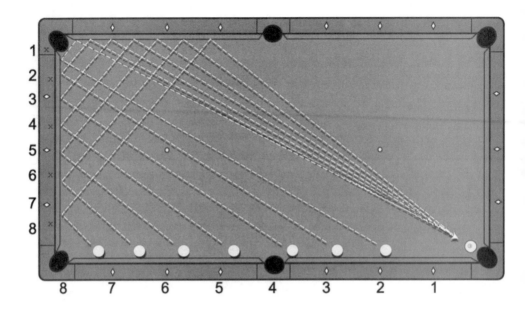

THE TWO RAIL CORNER SYSTEM

The above system is one of the easiest two rail systems to pocket the corner object ball. First, number the side rail diamonds 1 through 8. Next number each end rail 1/2 diamond 1 through 8 starting with the #1 diamond at the corner pocket. Now you simply connect like numbers. Place the cue ball close to the side rail cushion and in line with side rail diamond #1 and end rail diamond #1. Obviously you can't aim into the corner pocket so you aim about one inch in on the end rail cushion. Use a soft to moderate hit with high right english, and the cue ball will rebound off the two rail cushions back towards the object ball. Next, place the cue ball close to the side rail in line with side rail diamond #2 and end rail diamond #2. Again, use high right english with a soft to moderate stroke and the cue ball will rebound off the two rails towards the object ball. Continue to move up the side rail all the way to position #7. Notice the parallel track lines to the end rail cushion.

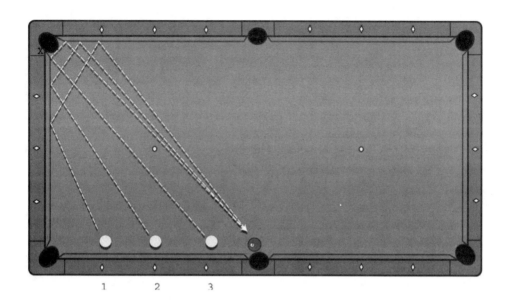

THE TWO RAIL SIDE POCKET KICK

The above diagram illustrates how a ball in front of the side pocket can be kicked in two rails from various cue ball positions on the table. When the cue ball is at diamond # 1 on the side rail, aim at the first diamond in on the end rail. Use a soft to moderate stroke with running (high & right) english and the cue ball will rebound off the two cushions towards the object ball in front of the side pocket. When the cue ball position moves up the side rail to diamond #2, the contact point on the end rail moves to about the 1/4 diamond point. Again, use a soft to moderate stroke with running english, and the cue ball will rebound off the two cushions towards the side pocket. When the cue ball position moves up to diamond #3, aim as close to the pocket as possible on the end rail cushion. Use a soft to moderate stroke but only use high english.

Practice all three of these shots using the donuts for a consistent set up. Once you become proficient in your execution, remove the donuts and practice shooting from various spots along the side rail. Just find the closest known track and parallel shift over to the cue ball. Do not move farther up the side rail than diamond #3. Moving past diamond #3 requires the use of inside or "hold" english which is very unpredictable. Also never hit this shot too hard because there is always the possibility of a scratch into the corner pocket.

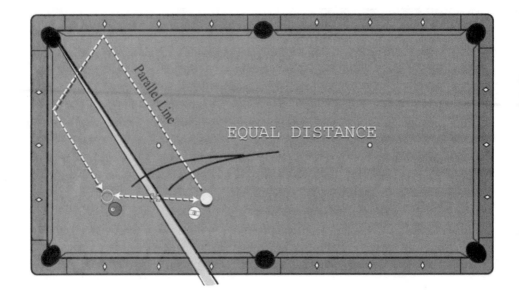

THE TWO RAIL DIRECT CORNER KICK

The above illustration seems to come up quite often while playing nine ball. First, extend the cue stick to the center of the corner pocket. Next, rotate the butt of the cue until it is equal distance between the cue ball and the ghost cue ball that will strike the object ball. You have now determined the midpoint between where your cue ball is and where you want it to end up. Many players think they know this simple system but make the crucial mistake by calculating the midpoint between the cue ball and the object ball. This usually results in too thin of a hit on the object ball or a complete miss hit resulting in a foul. Now you simply parallel shift the cue stick from its midpoint position to the pocket to directly over the cue ball to the cushion. You now have determined the contact point on the cushion where you must hit the cue ball for it to end up at the ghost cue ball position. Shoot the cue ball with a moderate stroke with running english.

The key to this corner kicking system is to always calculate the midpoint correctly and be sure you parallel shift with the cue stick accurately. Many players have a tendency to move one end of the cue stick more than the other. This always results in a miscalculation of the contact point on the cushion. This system also works best towards the end of the table. As the balls become separated more and move towards the center of the table, it is more difficult to judge the midpoint and to parallel shift the cue stick accurately.

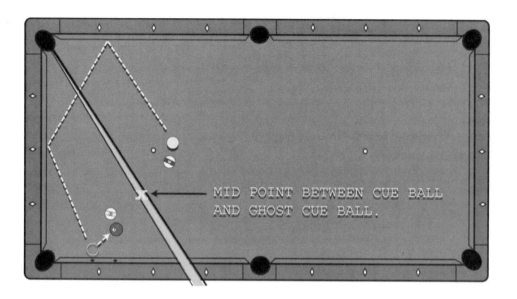

MID POINT BETWEEN CUE BALL
AND GHOST CUE BALL.

THE TWO RAIL INDIRECT CORNER KICK

The above illustration is almost identical to the previous one, but the direct two rail route to the object ball is blocked by another ball. The cue ball must come in from behind the object ball off the cushion for a legal hit. Again, the calculation of the ghost cue ball position and the midpoint is crucial. First, measure the distance from the object ball to the cushion. Now take this same distance down the cushion towards the corner pocket. This is the point on the cushion you want the cue ball to contact.

The easiest way to determine the ghost cue ball position is to place your thumb on the edge of the cushion directly across from the object ball and your index finger directly over the object ball. Now rotate your finger to the cushion while pivoting on your thumb. Be sure to keep the distance between your thumb and index finger the same as you rotate. Now place your finger on the cloth at the center of the ghost cue ball where it contacts the cushion. Place the tip of the cue stick at the center of the opposite corner pocket and rotate the butt end of the cue until it is equal distance between your finger (ghost cue ball) and the center of the cue ball.

You have now determined the midpoint between the two cue balls. Simply parallel shift the cue stick over the cue ball. The spot where the cue tip meets the cushion will be your contact point. Again, use running (high left) english on the cue ball with a moderate stroke, and the cue ball will come in behind the object ball as illustrated.

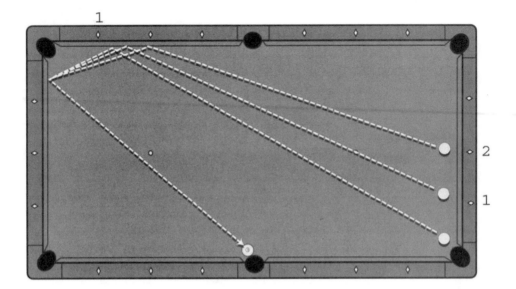

THE TWO RAIL SIDE POCKET KICK

The above diagram illustrates how an object ball can be kicked into the side pocket using various cue ball positions. The aiming point for the cue ball is diamond #1 on the side rail cushion for all three cue ball positions. Use a slow stroke for all three shots. This prevents the cue ball from scratching into the corner pocket after contact with the object ball. The only thing that varies is the amount of side spin applied to the cue ball.

When the cue ball is located in front of the corner pocket, use only a little high english and a slow stroke. As the cue ball moves in towards diamond #1 on the end rail, the cue ball rebound angle must be widened by applying high left english to the cue ball. And finally as the cue ball moves to diamond # 2, apply about 1 1/2 cue tips of left english to the cue ball and the cue ball will spin off the end rail cushion at a wider angle towards the object ball in front of the side pocket.

Another way to make this side pocket object ball from various cue ball positions is to vary the contact point on the side rail cushion. Again you know the line from the corner pocket to the diamond #1 on the side rail pockets the ball in front of the side pocket using a little high english and a slow stroke. If the cue ball moves left or right of this line, you just parallel shift the cue stick from the known line to the cue ball for your new line to the cushion. Again, use a slow stroke and a little high english. The triangle table diagram at the beginning of this chapter will help you visualize this shot.

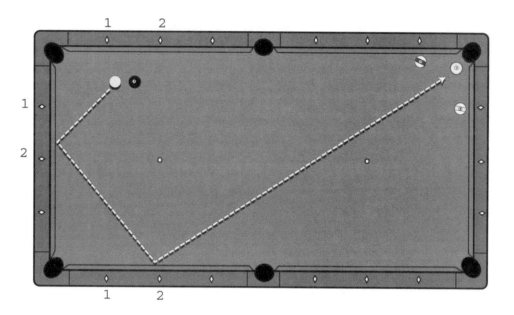

THE 2 TO 2 TO 2 CORNER KICK

This is a very easy connect-the-dots two rail kick. When the cue ball is in line with diamond #2 on the side rail and diamond #2 on the end rail, it will rebound off diamond #2 on the other side rail cushion towards the object ball in front of the corner pocket. Use a moderate stroke with a center to slightly above center cue ball hit.

If you need to kick at the object ball one diamond up on the side rail, your contact point on the end rail cushion moves 1/4 diamond forward of diamond #2. If you need to kick at the object ball one diamond out on the end rail, the contact point on the end rail cushion will move 1/4 diamond back from diamond #2.

These two rail kicks are basically a 4 to 1 ratio when moving away from the known kicking line. Moving the contact point on the end rail cushion 1/4 diamond will move the cue ball 1 whole diamond at the other end. Moving the cue ball contact point 1/2 diamond on the end rail cushion will move the cue ball 2 diamonds at the other end of the table.

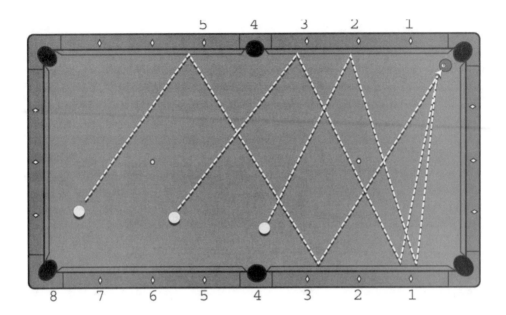

SIDE RAIL TWO RAIL KICKING

Side two rail kicking is only used as a last resort. It is very difficult to gauge and almost impossible to calculate. Virtually all of the outside factors will effect the final destination of the cue ball. These include the cleanliness of the cloth and balls, the type of cloth, the condition of the rails, the humidity in the room, etc. But the most important factor is the speed of the cue ball. Almost all side two rail kicks require a firm to very firm center ball hit on the cue ball. This will compress the cushion more than normal and alter the rebound angle. Second, the cue ball will acquire side spin from the cushion after it strikes the first rail. In the above illustration notice how the rebound angle of the cue ball is much less coming off the second rail than the first rail. This is due to the english the cue ball picks up after contact with the cushion.

Spend a little time practicing the above three shots. All of these require a fairly firm dead center ball hit on the cue ball. Be sure not to add any side spin or it will greatly affect the rebound angles. You should notice that all three shots require about the same speed. Next, experiment with moving the contact point on the cushion 1/4 diamond either way and either adding or subtracting to the speed of the cue ball. Remember, less speed widens the rebound angle and more speed shortens the angle. Spend only a short amount of time getting the feel for these shots. Again, these are very unpredictable and last resort shots.

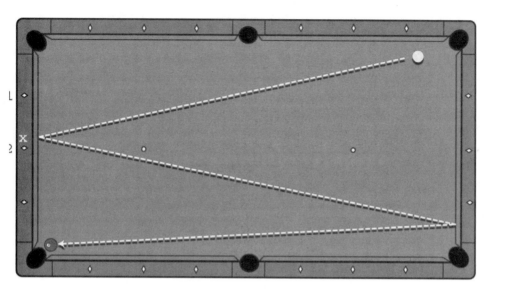

END RAIL TWO RAIL KICKING

This end rail two cushion kick is easier than it looks. First you start with a known track line. You know that coming out of the corner pocket to the middle diamond on the end rail cushion will put the cue ball into the opposite corner pocket. Now just back up about 1/4 diamond on the end rail cushion. The cue ball will rebound off the first end rail cushion and contact the second end rail cushion about at the 1/2 diamond spot. The cue ball will again rebound off this second cushion at a narrower angle towards the object ball in front of the far corner pocket.

Again, the speed of the cue ball is crucial on this shot. This shot needs to be hit just hard enough for the cue ball to go three table lengths and pocket the object ball. If it is hit too hard, both rebound angles will be narrowed, and the cue ball will contact the far end rail completely missing the object ball. Also the cue ball needs to be hit dead center or slightly above dead center. Any side spin on the cue ball will greatly effect the rebound angles.

Also like the long rail opposite english kick shown earlier, always err towards the pocket on the second rail. Again, the margin for error is about eight inches between the edge of the object ball and the rebounding trajectory line from the second end rail cushion towards the first diamond on the side rail that will pocket the object ball. Contacting the second end rail cushion too far away from the corner pocket will always result in a missed ball.

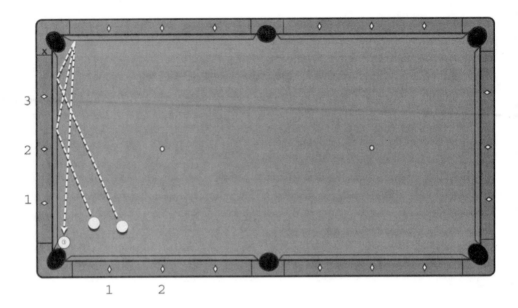

OPPOSITE ENGLISH TWO RAIL KICKING (SHORT)

Here again you assume your normal kicking angles are blocked. The goal is to force the cue ball away from its normal rebound path off the cushion. This is done with extreme opposite or inside english. When the cue ball is at diamond #1 on the side rail, aim at diamond #3 on the end rail with extreme (about 1 1/2 tips) of left english and a slow to moderate stroke. The "hold" english applied to the cue ball will cause it to rebound off the second rail back towards the object ball in front of the opposite corner pocket. As the cue ball moves up the side rail to about the 1 1/2 diamond position, aim for about the 3 3/4 diamond spot on the end rail with the same moderate stroke and extreme left english. Notice how this track line is virtually parallel to your original 1-3 track line. This shot becomes impossible as the cue ball location moves up the side rail past the 1 1/2 diamond location.

Again, do not spend much time practicing this shot. It is more important to know the theory on how and why it works and the limitations when it can be used. Inside or opposite english is always much more unpredictable than running english. The most important aspect of this shot is the speed of the cue ball. Too soft of a hit will cause the cue ball to rebound too sharply off the side rail cushion into the end rail cushion. Too much speed on the cue ball will cause it to go across the table towards the side rail away from the pocket.

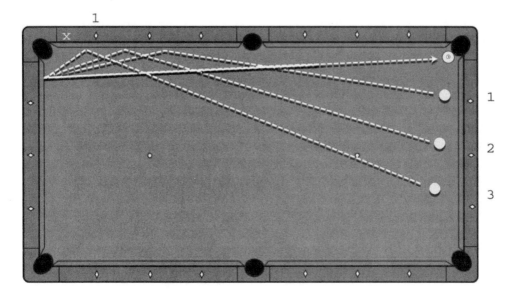

OPPOSITE ENGLISH TWO RAIL KICK (LONG)

The above illustrated opposite english hold kicks work the same on the long end rail as they do on the side rails. The key to these shots is a very firm loose stroke. It is almost like "throwing" the cue stick at the cue ball. An exaggerated follow through (12-16 inches) with the cue stick is needed to ensure the proper force and english is applied to the cue ball. Consider this stroke about a 3/4 break shot (see Chapter 8) stroke. This type of stroke ensures the cue ball will still have opposite spin when it contacts the end rail cushion because the side rail cushion will remove some of this needed spin.

When the cue ball is located at diamond #1 on the end rail, aim at the first diamond up from the corner pocket, applying high right english on the cue ball. With a firm loose stroke, the opposite english will spin the cue ball off the end rail cushion back towards the object ball in front of the corner pocket. As the cue ball moves to diamond #2 on the end rail, again aim at the first side rail diamond but only apply extreme (about 1 1/2 tips) right english. And finally as the cue ball moves to end rail diamond #3, apply the same extreme right english with a firm stroke but move the aiming point up the side rail to about the 1/2 diamond mark. Again, the cue ball will rebound off the end rail cushion back towards the object ball in front of the corner pocket. And like the other shots rebounding from the end rail cushion close to the pocket, always err with the cue ball approaching the side rail side of the pocket.

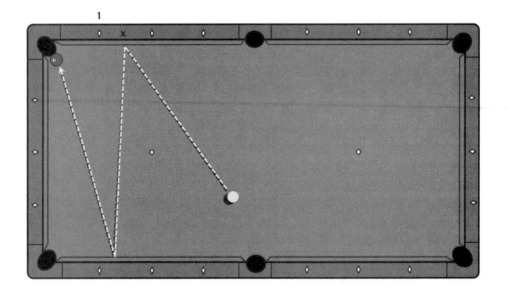

THE TWO RAIL HOLD AND RUNNING ENGLISH KICK

The above illustration is another last resort shot. The importance of this shot is to show that the same english applied to the cue ball can be both hold (opposite to the angle) and running (with the angle) on the same shot. Here the cue ball is in line with the side pocket and the 1 1/2 diamond mark on the opposite side rail. By striking the cue ball very firmly, the side rail cushion will be compressed and the rebound angle will be short-ened. By additionally adding low right english, this opposite spin will cause the angle to be shortened even more and the cue ball will almost rebound straight across the table. While much of this spin will dissipate after contact with the first cushion, the cue ball will still be spinning as it heads towards the opposite side rail. After contact with the second rail cushion, the cue ball will spin off the cushion at a wider rebound angle due to the running english spin on the cue ball towards the object ball in front of the corner pocket.

The key to this shot is the speed of the cue ball. The harder the cue ball is shot, the short-er both rebound angles will be. The slower the cue ball is shot, the wider both angles will be. This shot is also effected greatly by outside conditions. The cleanliness of the balls and cloth, the condition of the cloth and cushions, and the humidity in the room can virtually make these shots impossible.

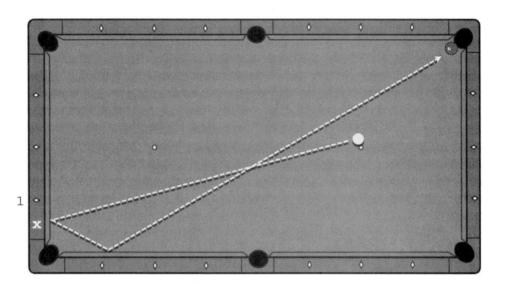

1

THE SPOT SHOT TWO RAIL CORNER KICK

When the cue ball is located about on the spot where the balls would normally be racked, an object ball can be pocketed in front of the corner pocket as indicated by the above illustration. Just aim at about the one half diamond mark on the end rail applying left english to the cue ball with a slow to moderate stroke, and the cue ball will spin off the two rails towards the corner pocket. If the cue ball is left or right of this known track line, just parallel shift the cue stick over to the cue ball, indicating the new contact point on the end rail cushion. Maximum amount of english is required for these shots so a good loose follow through stroke is a must. Striking the cue ball too hard will cause the cushions to be compressed more, and the rebound angle will be narrowed, causing the cue ball to contact the opposite end rail cushion away from the object ball.

THREE RAIL KICKING

Kicking three rails is very similar to two rail kicking. Just imagine the cue ball traveling a little farther, striking a third rail cushion and rebounding again. With what you learned with one and two rail kicking, you now probably have a very good idea of the third rail rebound angle. Almost all use a running english (a little high & side) hit on the cue ball. Understanding and memorization of the diamond system is a must for these kicks. Also the cue ball will usually be traveling great distances on most of these three rail kicks. It is therefore very important that you have developed a smooth, solid, good stroke from Chapters 1 & 2.

As you practice these kicks, you may even find them easier than some of the two rail kicks. In some cases, the margin for error is less on three rail kicks than the two rail kicks. In fact the first illustrated kick is what I call "The Most Forgiving Shot in Pool." This kick shot has a margin of error of almost 10 inches. I know of no other shot that can be made with this error margin. Learn these tracks as you practice the following illustrations. Then when you are in a game situation, again find the track you know and just parallel shift over to the cue ball.

After learning all of these 1, 2, & 3 rail kicking systems, giving up ball-in-hand on fouls will almost become a thing of the past. You should now be able to hit virtually any ball on the table. And don't be surprised if you even make some. Let your opponent be the surprised one. I knew you would like the "WORLD OF PARALLELS."

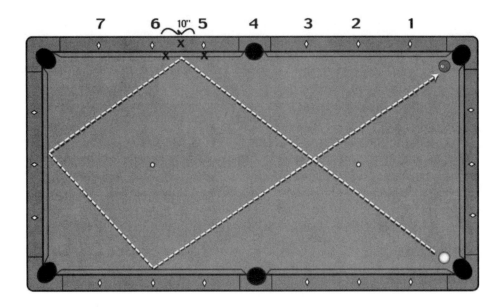

THE MOST FORGIVING 3 RAIL KICK SHOT IN POOL

On virtually all good tables, an object ball located in front of the corner pocket can be made very easily by the cue ball traveling three rails and coming out of the opposite corner pocket. The aiming spot on the side rail is about the 5 1/2 diamond spot. The cue ball should be struck with a soft to moderate stroke using running (high left) eng-lish. This will spin the cue ball three rails towards the corner pocket. If the aiming spot on the side rail is moved back on the cushion to directly across from the #5 diamond, the cue ball will actually travel four rails and contact the side rail cushion just before the object ball and rebound off the cushion, knocking the object ball into the pocket.

If the aiming point on the side rail is moved down the rail to diamond #6, the cue ball again will travel four rails, contacting the end rail cushion just before the object ball and rebound off the cushion knocking the object ball into the corner pocket. The distance between the spot on the cushion directly across from diamond #5 and the spot on the cushion directly in line with diamond #6 is about 10 inches. Remember, the distance between the spots on a nine foot table is 12 1/2 inches. This is why I call this shot The Most Forgiving Shot in Pool. I know of no other shot with an error margin of 10 inches. Even "C" players should make this shot 90% of the time.

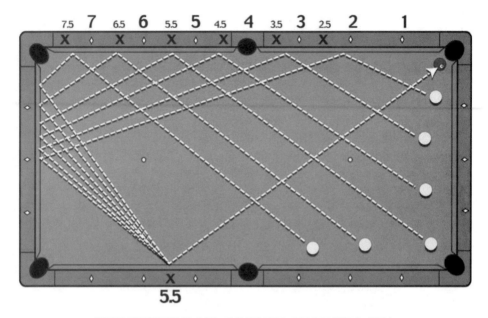

THE THREE RAIL CORNER KICK TRACKS

Although all those lines make this illustration look awfully complicated, it is much simpler than it looks. First, go back one page to the three cushion kick you just learned. Now come back to this diagram and find that same illustration. What this illustration shows is if the cue ball moves 1 diamond left or right of corner pocket, the contact point on the side rail cushion moves up or down one diamond. So if your normal contact point on the side rail from the corner pocket is the 5 1/2 diamond mark, your new reference point is the 4 1/2 or 6 1/2 diamond mark. If the cue ball moves 2 diamonds left or right of the corner pocket, your contact point on the cushion moves 2 diamonds from the original 5 1/2 diamond mark to the 3 1/2 or 7 1/2 diamond mark. Notice how all the paths to the first rail cushion from the various cue ball positions are all parallel. This shot is virtually a parallel shift from the corner pocket to the side rail 5 1/2 diamond mark to wherever the cue ball lies. Notice also that the contact point on the third rail cushion by the cue ball is about the 5 1/2 diamond mark for each of the shot variations.

Spend a little time practicing this shot. Once you have learned the theory behind this shot, it will only take a matter of minutes to execute this shot from anywhere between the various track lines. Again, use running (high left) english on the cue ball and a moderate stroke.

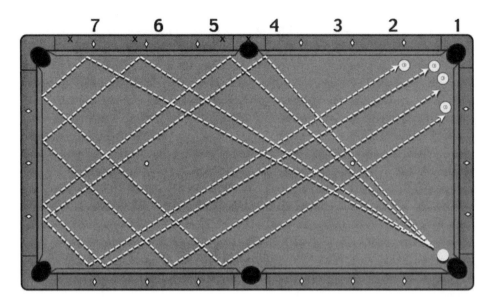

THREE RAIL KICKING AWAY FROM THE CORNER POCKET

Many times the object ball is not in the "jaws" of the corner pocket. In those cases, the contact point on the first side rail cushion must be adjusted up or down from your known track to effect the final destination of the cue ball. Always start with what you know. From the corner pocket to the side rail cushion at about diamond #5 1/2 puts the cue ball three rails into the opposite corner pocket on the end rail with running english. When the object ball is about one diamond up on the side rail from the corner pocket, the contact point on the first side rail cushion moves down to about diamond #4. When the object ball is only slightly up the side rail from the corner pocket, the contact point moves to about the 4 1/2 diamond mark.

If the object ball is about one diamond in from the corner pocket on the end rail, the contact point on the first side rail moves all the way up to about the 7 1/2 diamond mark. If the object ball is only slightly in from the corner pocket on the end rail, the contact point on the side rail cushion is about the 6 1/2 diamond mark. So now you have probably noticed your ratio on this shot is 2:1. Moving the contact point on the side rail cushion 2 diamonds moves the cue ball one diamond on its final three rail destination point. You will also notice as the object ball moves up the side rail, a softer hit on the cue ball is needed. As the object ball moves away from the pocket along the end rail cushion, a much firmer or harder hit is needed. Again, use a smooth stroke with running (high left) english.

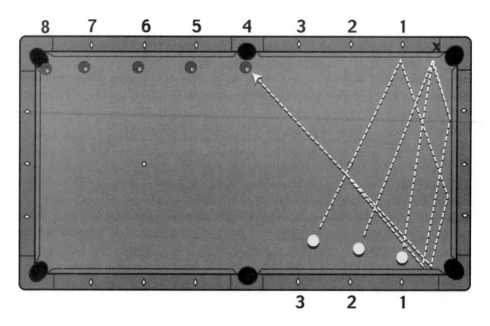

THE THREE RAIL SIDE POCKET KICK

Here your goal is to kick the object ball into the side pocket from various cue ball locations. The standard for this 3 rail side pocket kick is the 3:1 line. When the cue ball is at diamond #3 on the near side rail and in line with diamond #1 on the far side rail, the cue ball will travel 3 rails towards the object ball in front of the side pocket with a moderate to firm stroke and a dead center ball hit. As the cue ball moves down the side rail to diamond position #2, simply parallel shift the cue stick from the known 3:1 line over to the cue ball. This new line would put you directly into the corner pocket so just back up the cushion about 1 inch to the new contact point. Again, use a moderate to firm stroke and a dead center ball hit. If the cue ball is missing the object ball long in front of the side pocket, the cue ball is either being hit too softly or english (high, right, or both) is being applied to the cue ball. If the cue ball is missing the object ball short, the cue ball is being hit too hard or english (high, right, or both) is being applied to the cue ball. And finally as the cue ball moves to side rail diamond #1, aim for the same contact point as side rail diamond #2 but apply high right english to the cue ball.

Practice each of these shots. Once you obtain the feel for the necessary speed and english needed, practice kicking at the object balls on the far side rail at diamonds 5-8. Notice by varying the contact point on the first cushion, the speed of the cue ball, and the amount of english applied, almost all of these object balls can be hit from all three cue ball locations.

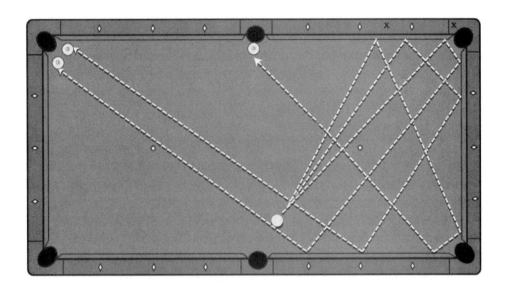

THREE RAIL KICKING FROM THE SIDE POCKET

When the cue ball is in front of the side pocket, an object ball can be kicked in 3 rails in front of the opposite side pocket or the corner pocket. For the side pocket kick, aim at the 1 1/2 diamond spot on the rail using a very firm stroke and a dead center ball hit on the cue ball. The firm stroke will compress the first cushion and shorten the rebound angle of the cue ball. The cue ball will then contact the end rail cushion at about the 1/4 diamond mark and rebound off the side rail cushion towards the side pocket.

For the three rail corner pocket kick, simply move the contact point on the side rail cushion down the rail towards the corner pocket and add side spin to the cue ball. Use a soft to moderate stroke and about one tip of right english. If the object ball is slightly up the side rail from the corner pocket, aim at the #1 diamond. The cue ball will travel three rails towards the side rail object ball. If the object ball is slightly away from the corner pocket on the end rail cushion, move the contact point on the first cushion to about one inch from the corner pocket. Again, the cue ball will travel three rails towards the object ball using a moderate stroke and about 1 tip of right english. These slightly away from the pocket kicks are usually best made when the cue ball actually contacts the 4th rail cushion first, slightly before the object ball.

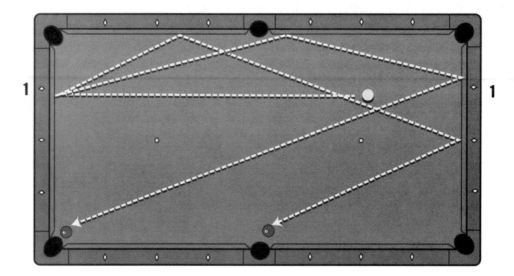

THE END RAIL THREE CUSHION SIDE/CORNER POCKET KICK

When the cue ball is in line with the end rail #1 diamond, an object ball in front of the illustrated side or corner pocket can be kicked in three rails. For the three rail corner pocket kick, shoot directly up the table towards the end rail diamond #1. Use a moderate to firm stroke and apply high right (about 1 o'clock) english to the cue ball. The key to this shot is for the cue ball to rebound off the end rail cushion and contact the side rail cushion just past the side pocket. If the side pocket keeps getting in the way while practicing this shot, just add a little more speed to the cue ball to lessen the rebound angle off of the end rail cushion. If the cue ball is contacting the side rail cushion too far down the rail towards the corner pocket, add more side spin or reduce the cue ball speed.

The side pocket three rail kick is shot the same way as the corner pocket kick shot except a little more side spin (about 2 o'clock) is added to the cue ball. Again, use a firm to moderate stroke and the cue ball will rebound off the end rail cushion towards the first diamond up from the side pocket. It will then rebound off the side rail cushion towards the end rail cushion at about the middle diamond and rebound towards the object ball in front of the side pocket. If you fail to make the object ball into the side pocket, make the same adjustments as above by altering the amount of side spin applied to the cue ball or the cue ball speed.

FOUR RAIL KICKING

The following illustrated four rail examples are only used as a last resort. These four rail kicks usually only work when there are very few balls on the table because the cue ball must travel a great distance around the table. The most common example is when a small cluster of balls surrounds the cue ball blocking all other kicking paths to the object ball. A very firm smooth loose stroke is necessary for all of these kicks. An erratic stroke or contact of the cue tip to the cue ball at any place on the cue ball other than it was intended will cause the cue ball path to be greatly altered.

If you have to use one of these illustrated four rail kicking examples to hit the object ball, you probably should jump or masse the cue ball or take a deliberate foul by tying up two or more of the blocking object balls. Basically, these are fun shots to be used in fun situations.

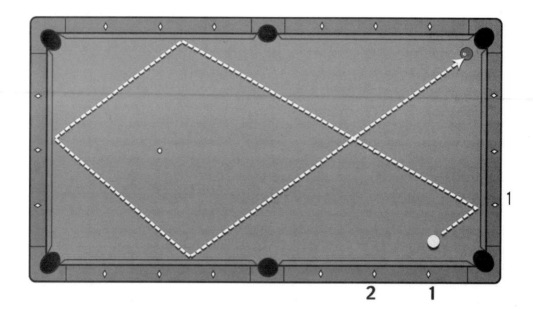

THE 2 TO 1 FOUR RAIL CORNER KICK

Here assume a cluster of balls is surrounding the cue ball blocking all easier kicking paths to the object ball in front of the corner pocket. The cue ball is directly in line with the side rail #2 diamond and the end rail #1 diamond. You know from the one rail kicking section that this line will put the cue ball into the side pocket using high left english. So all you need to do is remove the side spin from the cue ball, and the cue ball will hit farther down the side rail cushion towards diamond #6. It will continue two more rails towards the object ball in front of the corner pocket. Perhaps you have already noticed that after the cue ball rebounds off the first end rail cushion, this shot is only a variation of the three rail kick shot discussed in the previous section. Use a very firm smooth loose stroke with about 1 tip of high english.

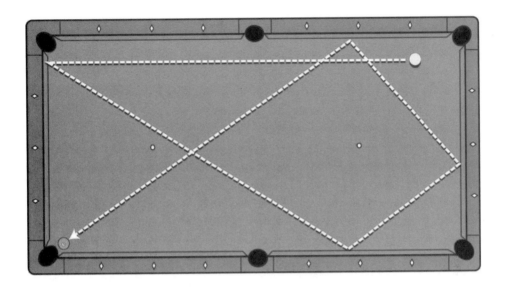

THE ENGLISH END RAIL 4 RAIL CORNER KICK

Here again you assume a cluster of balls is blocking all normal paths to the object ball. Your only option is straight up the table. The first thing you do is walk to the other end of the table and notice that your contact point on the end rail cushion is only an inch or so away from the corner pocket. You know with what you learned in the three rail section that the cue ball coming out of this corner pocket into the side rail diamond 5-6 with running english will pocket the object ball in the opposite corner pocket. So now all you need to do is get the cue ball to rebound off the end rail cushion towards about the side rail 5 1/2 diamond mark. This is accomplished by striking the cue ball firmly with extreme (about 1 1/2 tips) left english. The cue ball will spin off the end rail cushion and proceed in the three rail kicking tracks towards the object ball in the corner pocket. You will need a very loose fluid forceful stroke to accomplish the desired result. If you are unable to make the corner ball, try moving your contact point on the end rail cushion towards the first diamond.

I have several words of caution on this shot. If your cue stick has a lot of deflection and since the cue ball is being struck very firmly and away from the center, the cue ball can actually "squirt" directly into the corner pocket. You may need to actually aim several inches out from the corner pocket to compensate for this squirt. Much more will be discussed on this subject in chapter 13.

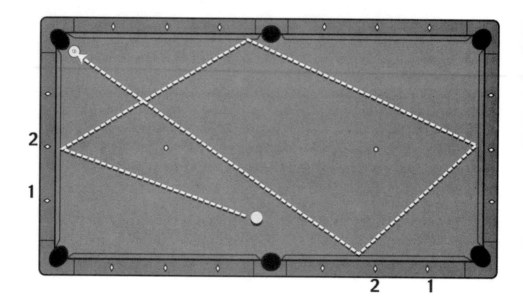

THE 2 TO 2 FOUR RAIL CORNER KICK

This is another one of those shots that looks harder than it is. Again, assume a cluster of balls surrounds the cue ball blocking all other paths to the object ball in front of the corner pocket. Here the cue ball is directly in line with both the side rail diamond #2 and the end rail diamond #2. By aiming into the end rail cushion at the middle diamond mark and applying running (high right) english to the cue ball, the cue ball will go four rails towards the object ball in front of the corner pocket.

There are two key factors to this shot. First, a firm loose smooth stroke is required. An erratic stroke will alter the cue ball path. Second, the proper amount of right english must be applied to the cue ball so it contacts the first side rail cushion slightly before the side pocket. Again, you probably have noticed that after the cue ball rebounds off the first end rail cushion, this shot is just another variation of the three rail kick shot discussed at the beginning of the three rail kicking section.

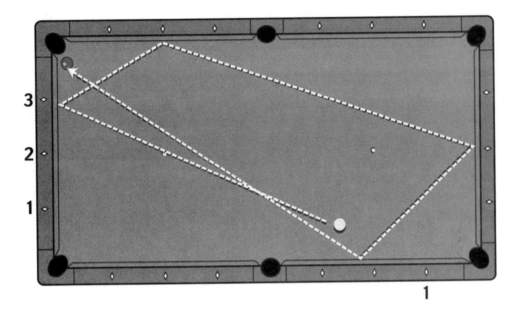

1

THE 1 TO 3 FOUR RAIL KICK

This kick is more natural and easier than the previous illustrated example. It is just a parallel shift over from the previous 2-2 line, and you don't have to worry about the scratch into the side pocket. When the cue ball is in line with diamond #1 on the side rail and diamond #3 on the end rail, aim at the end rail diamond #3 with a firm stroke and about 1 tip of high english. The cue ball will rebound off the end rail cushion and go four rails towards the object ball in the corner pocket.

The difficulty of this shot in game situations is that in many cases, the obstructing ball(s) are also in the way of the cue ball as it rebounds off the fourth side rail towards the object ball. Notice how the beginning of the cue ball path is very similar to its ending path. In many cases, a slight shift either left or right of diamond #3 will be needed to slightly alter the cue ball path away from the obstructer ball(s). This will cause the cue ball to contact either the side or end rail cushion first just before the object ball. The cue ball will then rebound off the final cushion towards the object ball knocking it into the corner. This actually turns into a five rail kick shot.

The key to this shot is avoiding the obstructer ball(s). First, always stand behind the object ball and determine the contact point of the cue ball off the fourth rail cushion that will be needed to avoid the obstructer ball(s). Then make the adjustment either left or right of diamond #3 on the end rail.

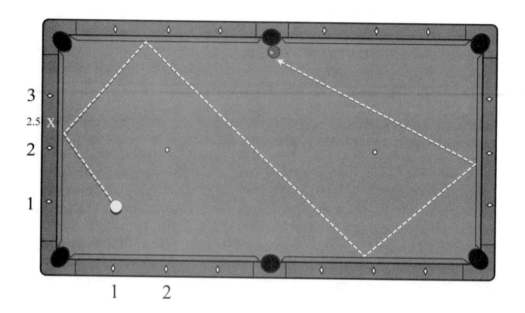

THE FOUR RAIL SIDE POCKET KICK

This kick is really a last resort shot. The cue ball is directly in line with the side rail diamond #2 and about the end rail 2 1/2 diamond mark. Aim directly into the end rail cushion at the 2 1/2 diamond mark with running (high right) english. Use a very forceful firm loose level stroke and the cue ball will travel four rails towards the object ball in front of the side pocket. The key to this shot is a hard level stroke. Because of the force the cue ball must be struck, a non-level stroke will invariably cause the cue ball to leave the table.

Notice on this shot how the cue ball takes some unnatural angles as it rebounds from the cushions. This is because the running english applied to the cue ball will actually be opposite or "holding" english when it strikes the third and fourth rails (almost all of the applied english will be dissipated before the cue ball contacts the fourth rail). Second, because of the force and angle the cue ball contacts the cushions, the cue ball will "slide" several inches as it rebounds away from the cushion. And finally, the cushions themselves will apply some spin to the cue ball. All of these will contribute to the erratic rebound nature of the cue ball off the cushions. This shot is also greatly affected by the various outside factors such as the cleanliness of the balls and cloth, responsiveness of the cushions, and the humidity in the room. Again, let me repeat that this is a last resort shot like all four rail kick shots.

Chapter Five
Banking

Banking is probably the most difficult aspect of the game. The same external factors (speed, english, humidity, cleanliness, etc.) that affect the kicking game can be compounded even more while banking. Understanding the table and the diamond system discussed in Chapter 4 is absolutely necessary before you can improve your banking skills.

Most banks can be calculated and pocketed using the simple diamond system and parallel shifting to the cue ball. Banking is also more difficult than kicking in that you must hit the cue ball into the object ball to a calculated spot on the cushion. With kicking you only have to hit the calculated spot on the first cushion with the cue ball. The following theories and examples will vastly improve your banking skills. Because of its difficulty, banking requires more practice than any other aspect of the game (except the stroke builders). It has been said that some of the top professionals do not know or use some of these theories. They have basically learned banking by "rote". That is to say they have learned by memory without thought of meaning. They know the how but not the why by spending countless hours practicing over their lifetime. By understanding the following theories and practicing the illustrations, you can become much more proficient at this aspect of the game in much less time than it took some of the professionals to learn by trial and error.

The best way to shoot a bank shot along its calculated banking line is to use high english on the cue ball and a fairly soft stroke. This will allow for the least amount of "slide" by the cue ball and give the truest roll of both balls. Second, the softer hit will cause the least compression of the cushion giving the truest rebound angle off the calculated banking point on the cushion. Always shoot banks this way when the only goal is to make the object ball. The only negative on this high english banking is it will cause the cue ball to roll forward. Always be cognizant of the tangent rebound angle of the cue ball off the object ball to be sure it also will not find a pocket to scratch in.

With all that said, you may have noticed many of the better banking players prefer to hit the object ball harder and with a center to slightly below center ball hit on the cue ball. They feel they can be more accurate with a lesser rebound angle caused by the more forceful stroke. Also since they are stroking the cue ball harder, the slightly below center hit on the cue ball will keep it from running around the table looking for a hole to scratch in. And many of these players "grew up" playing on inferior equipment (bad cloth, dead rails, non-level tables, out of round balls, etc.) that would effect the roll of a slow rolling ball. They would constantly get upset when the table conditions would effect their bank shots. So because they learned their own banking system early on, they continue to use it today even with the best equipment. And some players will move the banking point down even farther on the cushion and apply inside (hold) english on the object ball. This running english applied to the cue ball will transfer a little opposite spin to the object ball, further narrowing the release angle from the cushion. Again, these players feel they can be even more accurate with a straighter release angle to the pocket.

Practice the following illustrations with different speeds and english. You will be amazed how much you can affect the path of the object ball. This is why in banking it is paramount to calculate and hit the correct contact point on the cushion and to stroke the cue ball with a slightly above center cue ball hit. Now you see why Rule #3 of the "Winning Rules For Nine Ball" is so important when playing nine ball.

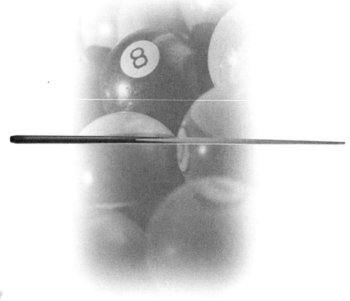

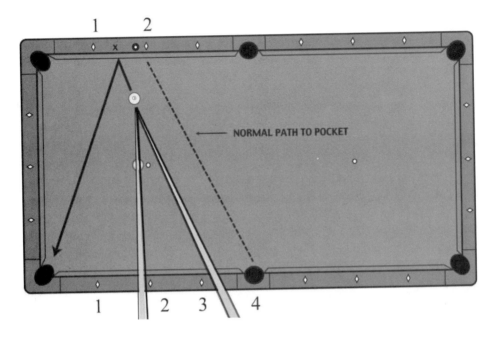

BASIC BANKING THEORY

From what you learned from the diamond system in chapter #4, you simply start with what you know. You know the line from the center of the side pocket (diamond #4) to the side rail diamond #2 takes you to the opposite corner pocket. Take the cue stick and hold it over this line. Now parallel shift the cue stick to the object ball placing the tip on the cloth just outside the center ball edge of the object ball. The cue stick is now pointing at the contact point on the cushion where the object ball must contact to be banked into the corner pocket. Now rotate the butt end of the cue stick (don't move the tip) to directly over the cue ball. Notice the point on the side rail where the butt end of the cue stick crosses the side rail, the spot on the opposite rail where the cue stick is pointing, and the contact point on the object ball. Connecting these three points or dots will give you the new shooting line.

Shooting this shot with a soft to moderate stroke and a high english hit on the cue ball will bank the object ball into the corner pocket. Shooting this bank with a firmer hit and a little low english will compress the cushion farther resulting in a lesser rebound angle. The contact point on the cushion must be moved down farther towards the pocket to compensate for the reduced rebound angle. Applying low left (inside) english to the cue ball will cause the cushion contact point to be moved even closer to the pocket.

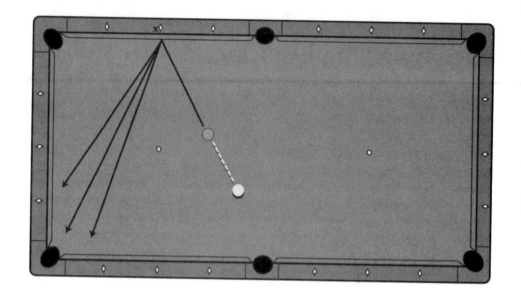

THE IMPORTANCE OF SPEED ON BANKS

The above illustration shows a "dead" bank into the corner pocket. Both the cue ball and object ball are directly in line with the side pocket and a spot on the opposite side rail slightly down from the diamond #2 (the half way point). Shooting this shot with a high english hit on the cue ball and a moderate stroke will pocket the object ball into the corner pocket. If you aim at the same spot on the cushion but shoot the bank very softly, the cushion will compress very little and the object ball will bank wide towards the end rail. On the other hand, a very firm hit on the cue ball will greatly compress the cushion and lessen the rebound angle causing the object ball to be banked towards the side rail.

This is why the best bank pool players in the world use a consistent speed and cue ball hit on every shot. This consistency gives them a predictable outcome. Unless you must "throw" the bank with english or need the cue ball to travel to a designated spot, shoot each bank with a consistent soft to moderate stroke and an above center cue ball hit.

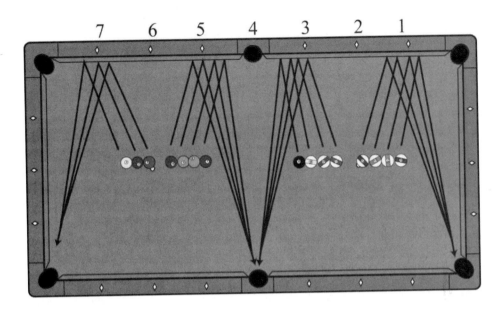

THE BEST BANKING EXERCISE DRILL

This is by far the best banking exercise drill you can practice. Line up all fifteen balls down the center of the table as illustrated. With ball-in-hand on each shot, bank each ball into the designated pocket. Start at one end of the table and work towards the other end. Use a fluid soft to moderate stroke. Strike the cue ball about 1/4 tip above dead center with a consistent stroke on each shot. The high english on the cue ball and the softer stroke will give the truest object ball roll both before and after the cushion. Your goal is to make all 15 balls with less then 20 attempts. This will give you a 75%-90% accuracy range on these shots.

There are three keys to the execution of these shots. First, properly parallel shift to the object ball from the known banking line using the diamonds on both sides of the table. Notice how all the lines to the cushion from the object balls are almost parallel to each other. Second, be sure to place the cue ball directly on this new line. And finally, use a consistent soft to moderate stroke. Working on this drill one hour a day for one week can definitely get you in the high percentage accuracy range on these shots. Repetitive practice on this drill will have you visualizing and memorizing these track lines so they will become second nature in game situations.

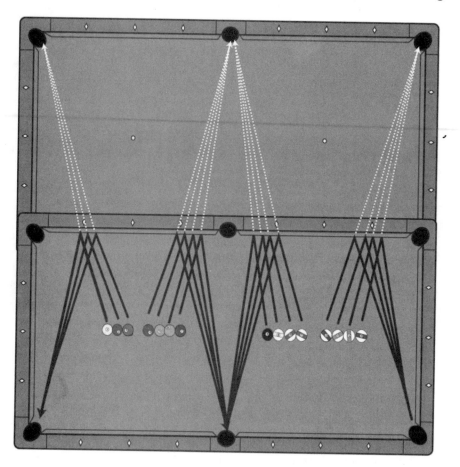

VISUALIZATION BANKING

The bottom diagram is an exact duplication of the previous page. But assume that instead of banking the object ball into the side rail cushion, there is no cushion and the table is extended widthwise one more table width. Notice how each of the object balls would proceed across both tables and pocket straight into the "ghost" table pockets. I like to use this system only as a secondary verification to the calculation from the known banking lines and parallel shifting. What you do here is measure the distance with the cue stick from the pocket you want to make the object ball across the table to within one ball width from the cushion. Jack Kohler, in his book "The Science of Pocket Billiards" explains why it is not an actual cushion to ghost table cushion measurement. Now duplicate this distance in a straight line farther out from the table. Vertically place the cue stick on the floor to this point. The spot on the cushion/rail directly in line with the cue stick and the object ball is the banking aiming point.

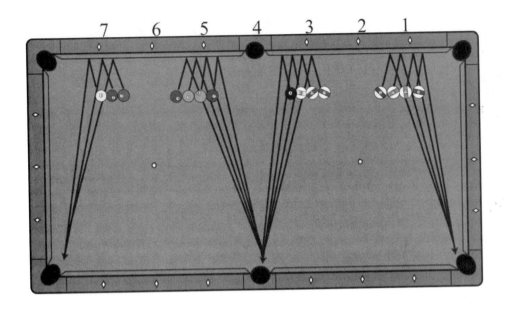

CLOSE TO THE CUSHION BANKING

This is the same drill as the BEST BANKING EXCERCISE DRILL except the object balls are close to the side rail cushion. As you learned early in the book, the cue ball first slides before it picks up forward roll after contact with the cue tip. The same thing happens with the object ball. As the cue ball contacts the object ball and transfers its energy, the object ball will slide a little before the friction of the cloth causes it to roll forward. This slide distance is mostly dependent on the velocity the object ball is struck as well as the cleanliness of the balls and cloth. The harder the object ball is struck and the cleaner or newer the balls and cloth are (less friction), the farther the object ball will slide before rolling forward.

In the BEST BANKING EXCERCISE DRILL illustration, the object balls were in the middle of the table and therefore rolling forward upon contact with the cushion. Here the object balls are close to the cushion. If these bank shots are hit firmly, the object ball will still be sliding upon contact with the cushion. As you might expect, balls rolling into the cushion will rebound slightly differently than balls sliding into the cushion. These sliding object balls close to the cushion will rebound at a slightly narrower angle. Therefore after your parallel shift from the known banking line to the object ball, the cushion contact point must be moved slightly farther down the rail. A slower cue ball hit can reduce some of the object ball slide.

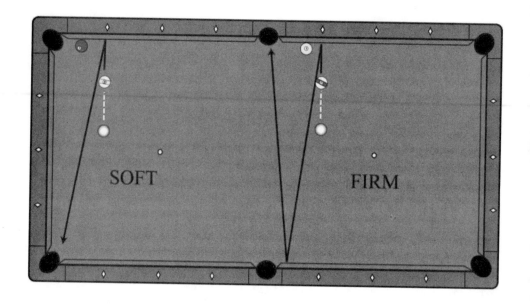

SOFT   FIRM

ENGLISH THROW BANKS

In the above illustration, the normal paths of both bank shots are blocked by another obstructer object ball. You are virtually limited to hitting the object ball straight into the rail. Without altering the object ball rebound angle, it will rebound straight back into the cue ball. But by applying low right english to the cue ball, the object ball path can be altered. First the object ball will be "thrown" slightly to the left because of the right spin on the cue ball. More will be discussed on this in later chapters. Second, the right spin on the cue ball will transfer some left spin to the object ball. Now the object ball is heading towards the rail at a slight angle and with some left spin. This will cause the object ball to spin off the cushion away from the cue ball towards the pocket.

For the corner pocket shot on the left, the object ball is hit softly allowing for the widest rebound angle. Use low right english on the cue ball. A soft hit will move the rebound angle of the object ball about one diamond. For the side pocket bank, use the same amount of low right english but use a firmer hit. This will compress the cushion farther and shorten the rebound angle causing the object ball to be banked two rails into the side pocket. Knowing this shot is extremely important when playing the game of one pocket.

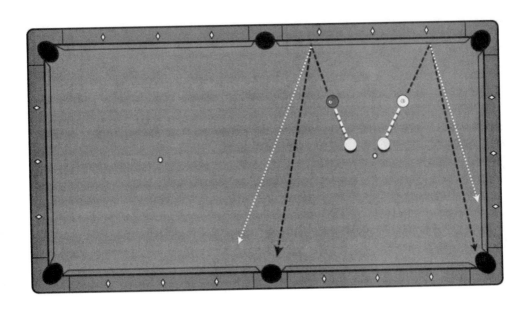

HOLD ENGLISH BANKING

In the above two examples, banking the object ball straight into the cushion will cause both banks to go wide of the pocket (dotted line). In the previous page illustration you needed to expand or widen the rebound angle of the object ball off the rail. Here if you do not alter your contact point on the cushion, the rebound angle of the object ball off the cushion must be narrowed to pocket the object ball. This can be accomplished by applying low left english on the cue ball for the side pocket bank. This will transfer right english to the object ball. This opposite (opposite to the direction of the traveling ball) or "hold" english will narrow the rebound angle of the object ball off the cushion and send it towards the pocket away from its natural rebound line. The corner pocket bank is shot the same way except low right english is applied to the cue ball. This will transfer left or "hold" english to the object ball narrowing the rebound angle of the object ball off the cushion.

Practice both of these banks as well as the previous page. Then go back to "THE BEST BANKING EXERCISE DRILL" and practice this same drill altering the cushion contact point, inside or outside english on the cue ball and the speed of the shot. Notice how the cushion contact point of the object ball can be varied several inches and still be made by varying the speed and english applied to the cue ball. I suggest in game situations only alter these shots if necessary. Otherwise, always parallel shift from the known banking line and use a consistent slightly above center cue ball hit.

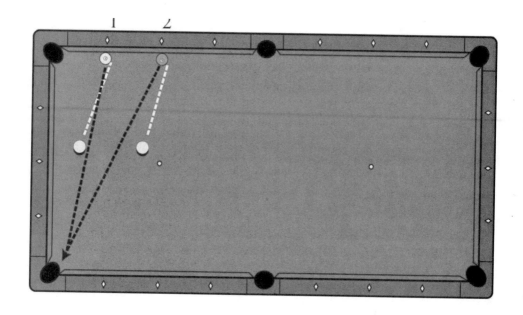

CUE BALL BELOW THE OBJECT BALL BANKING
(BACKWARDS BANKING)

This is another system that is quite accurate when the cue ball is below the object ball and the object ball is close to the cushion. Although I normally prefer the parallel shift to the object ball from the known banking line, sometimes it is difficult to establish that line on these shots. Usually these "backwards" banks are fairly thin hits on the object ball, making it difficult to determine the contact point of the cue ball on the object ball. When the object ball is at diamond #1 or below along the side rail cushion and the cue ball is below the object ball, aim the center of the cue tip at the edge of the object ball. The object ball will be banked back into the corner pocket. As the object ball moves up to about the second diamond, aim the center of the cue tip just outside the edge of the object ball. Again, the object ball will be banked back into the corner pocket.

These shots are normally shot with a little high english (top spin) on the cue ball and a slower than normal hit. This will allow the object ball to roll towards the pocket, eliminating some of the slide rebounding away from the rail. Also on this shot be careful of the scratch in the corner pocket. This pocket sure seems to suck up the cue ball quite often (OUCH!) on these backward bank shots.

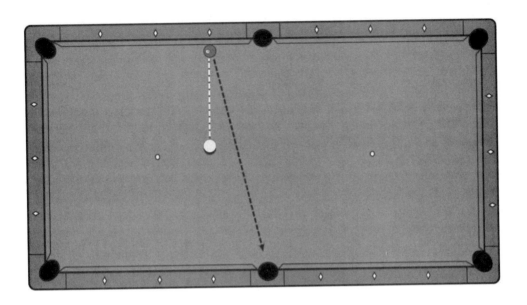

THE STRAIGHT ON FROZEN RAIL BANK

At first glance, the above side pocket bank shot looks impossible. Since the object ball is frozen to the cushion, the cue ball will not get out of the way fast enough as the object ball rebounds from the cushion. Right? Not necessarily. If you move the contact point farther outside the object ball, the cue ball will have a better chance of missing the rebounding object ball. Unfortunately, this will widen the rebound angle of the object ball causing it to go wide of the pocket. Therefore, the rebound angle of the object ball must be altered back towards the pocket. The following two things must be done to alter this rebound angle:

1) The cue ball must be hit very firmly. This firm hit will cause maximum compression of the cushion by the object ball, creating some distance between the cue ball and the rebounding object ball.

2) Extreme (about 1 1/2 tips) of right english will need to be applied to the cue-ball. This will result in left (hold) english transferred to the object ball narrowing the rebound angle.

Shoot this shot using a very smooth firm loose stroke and about a half ball hit on the object ball. Aim for a slightly fuller hit as due to the hard hit and extreme english, the cue ball will "squirt" (Chapter 13) slightly left.

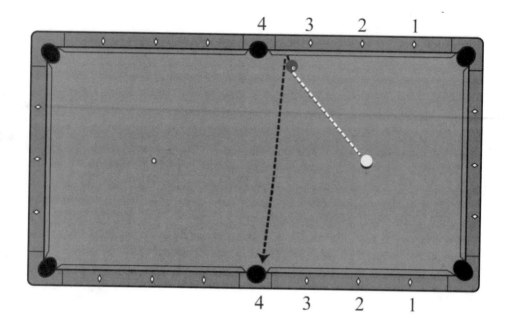

THE ACROSS TO THE SIDE POCKET BANK

This is another one of those shots that occurs fairly often. It is also easier than it looks. First, the margin for error is quite large on this shot. Since the object ball is rebounding off the cushion almost straight across the table, the full width (about 5 1/2 inches on a 9 foot table) of the large side pocket is available. That's almost a 2 1/2 ball margin of error. Second, if the ball is banked slightly short, it will normally go two rails back into the other side pocket. Determine the object ball contact point from your normal parallel shift from the closest known banking line. In this case, it would be the 2 to 3 line.

Shoot this shot with a nice soft to moderate stroke and about one tip of high english. The cue ball will rebound off the object ball into the side rail cushion and then rebound towards the end rail cushion. A double kiss on the cue ball is always caused by too full of a hit on the object ball. And always err to the short (right) side of the pocket as a miss can result in a two cushion bank to the other side pocket.

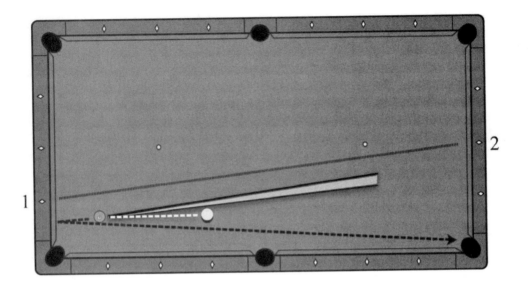

LONG RAIL BANKING

Long rail banking is much more difficult than side rail banking. There is very little margin for error. First, both the cue ball and object ball are traveling farther distances. The greater the distance, the more any error is magnified. Second, the available pocket width is almost always smaller. In the above example, the available pocket width is only about 3 inches (remember the corner pocket width is about 4 5/8 inches straight on) because of the angle to the pocket. The side rail cushion will block part of the pocket opening. Now remember the balls are 2 1/4 inches in diameter. Trying to get this 2 1/4 inch ball into a 3 inch opening after it has traveled 10 feet is not an easy shot. It is not an easy shot shooting straight on, let alone banking it off a cushion almost 9 feet away. This is why when playing a safety in nine ball, leaving your opponent a long rail bank is not a bad percentage play.

With all that said, these shots can still be made. Again, always start with what you know. The closest known banking line to the corner pocket is the 2 to 1 line. Now parallel shift the cue stick to the object ball as always and rotate the butt end over the cue ball. This is your new shooting line to the object ball to bank it into the corner pocket. These long rail banks are normally best shot by moving the contact point on the cushion slightly towards the pocket and applying inside (left) english to the cue ball. This will transfer right (outside, hold) english to the object ball allowing for narrower rebound angle off the cushion. Again, many players prefer a straighter rebound line to the pocket. Use a consistent loose fluid stroke.

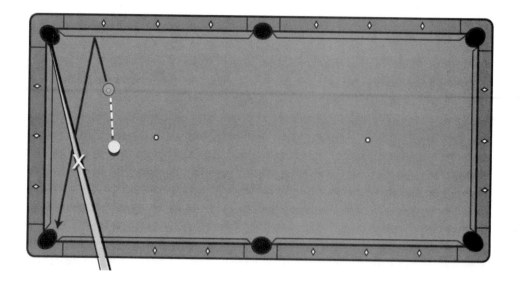

THE MIDPOINT BANKING SYSTEM

Although I normally prefer using the known diamond banking lines, this system also works very well especially when the banking angle is narrow (2 diamonds or less). This system works exactly like the midpoint kicking system discussed in Chapter 4. But instead of determining the midpoint between the cue ball and the object ball to be kicked, the banking midpoint is half way between the object ball and the pocket ("x" on the diagram). Now align the cue stick to the center of the opposite pocket (the pocket directly across the table from the pocket where you want the object ball to go) directly over the established mid point. This is your banking line to the pocket. Parallel shift the cue stick from this line to the object ball. Place the tip of the cue stick on the cloth slightly outside the center edge of the object ball and rotate the butt end over the cue ball. As before, line up the spot on the rail the cue tip is pointing, the contact point on the object ball, and the spot on the rail where the butt of the cue stick crosses. This is the new banking line for the object ball to be pocketed one rail into the corner pocket. Use a soft to moderate stroke and a high english cue ball hit.

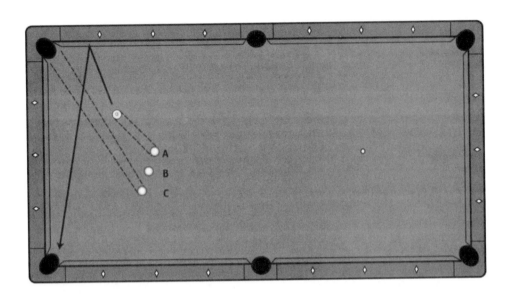

THE DREADED KISS ZONE

When the cue ball is above the object ball, many times the rebounding banked object ball will collide (kiss) the caroming cue ball as it rebounds off the cushion. The determining factor in avoiding this second collision is how much of the pocket you are shooting towards can be seen. At position "A" in the above diagram, the cue ball and object ball are lined up directly into the pocket. If you were to get very low on the shot and aim to make the cue ball directly into this pocket, the object ball would almost completely block your vision of the pocket. At cue ball position "C", the object ball is not in the way of the cue ball path towards this pocket. The cue ball could easily be shot directly into this pocket. At both positions "A" and "C", the object ball can be banked without "kissing" the cue ball as it rebounds from the cushion with a moderate slightly above center cue ball hit.

Cue ball position "B" is always the problem area. Here the object ball is blocking part of cueball path towards the pocket. Only part of the pocket is visible. Trying to bank the object ball into the corner pocket with a center ball hit and a moderate stroke will almost always cause the cue ball to collide with the object ball as they both rebound from the cushions. The only way to avoid this collision is to alter the cue ball path. This can be done by applying extreme side spin to the cue ball. This will cause the cue ball to rebound from the cushion at a different angle and possibly miss the object ball. Careful, as this spin will also transfer to the object ball altering its rebound path and making the bank even more difficult.

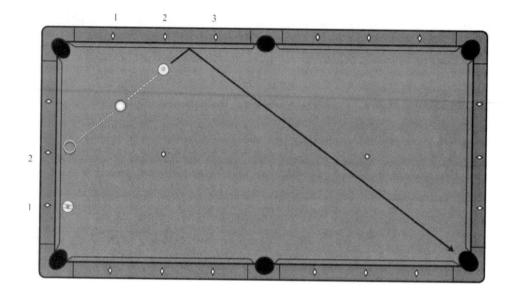

THE ONE RAIL BANK/SAFETY

The above shot seems to come up too often while playing nine ball. Due to bad position play, you are left with a long cut shot on the eight ball. Invariably the eight ball is missed and left in the jaws of the pocket for an easy sell out. Another way to approach this shot is a bank/safety. From Chapter 4 you know the line from the end rail middle diamond to the side rail diamond #3 puts you into the corner pocket. Use a soft stroke with extreme low english and draw the cue ball back to the end rail cushion. The object ball will be banked one rail into the corner pocket. If you miss the bank, try to err towards the side rail side. This will cause the missed object ball to rebound off the side rail cushion and end up on the end rail cushion. Now you have left your opponent with a very difficult shot as both the cue ball and eight ball are on the end rail cushions at opposite ends of the table. This is usually far better than the eight ball left in the jaws of the pocket on the missed cut shot.

The keys to this shot are to be sure the cue ball is drawn back to the end rail cushion. Second, the eight ball needs to be hit just hard enough so it remains close to the end rail cushion if missed. Missing towards the end rail usually leaves the object ball close to the pocket for a possible sell out. Spend a few minutes practicing this shot. Deliberately shoot the bank both towards the end rail and side rail while noticing where the object ball ends up each time.

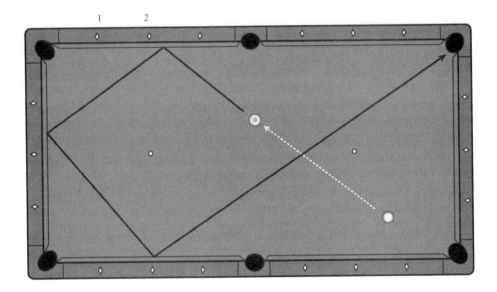

THE 3 RAIL CORNER POCKET BANK

When the object ball is in line with diamond #2 on the side rail and the opposite rail corner pocket, it can be banked three rails into the corner pocket as illustrated. Use a firm stroke and a slightly above dead center ball hit on the cue ball. This shot is used quite often when playing one pocket. Notice how the track lines run parallel to almost form a perfect square. The perfect square is compromised by the english applied to the object ball from the cushion, altering the rebound angle of the object ball as it rebounds away from the cushion. Also the object ball will "slide" a little as it rebounds from the cushion before picking up the forward roll. This sliding of the object ball will further cause the object ball path to be altered.

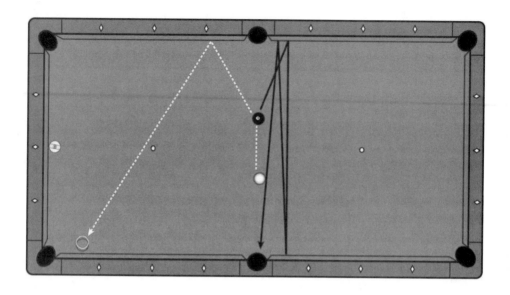

THE THREE RAIL SIDE POCKET BANK

Here you unfortunately are straight on the eight ball into the side pocket with the cue ball and the nine ball is on the far end cushion. The proper way to shoot this shot is to "cheat" the eight ball towards the right side of the pocket (remember these pockets are almost 2 1/2 balls wide). You can either "stun" the cue ball straight down the table with a very forceful center cue ball stroke or follow the cue ball into the cushion slightly left of the pocket with high left english, and the cue ball will spin off the side rail cushion towards the end rail.

But there is a third way to shoot this ball. Aim the eight ball into the rail about 1 1/2 inches up from the side pocket. Like the "stun" shot, use a very forceful stroke. The eight ball will bank off the cushion towards the other side rail. It will then rebound off this cushion back towards the side pocket or to a point on the cushion close to the side pocket. It will then rebound off this cushion back towards the other side pocket. This reversing of the angle is caused by the english the eight ball picks up from the cushions. The forceful hit also narrows the rebound angle. Use high right english on the cue ball. This reverse english will "hold" the cue ball allowing it to drift towards the end rail as it rebounds off the side rail cushion. Use this shot only in fun situations or possibly when you are trying to hustle someone. Your opponent will probably think it was just a lucky shot!

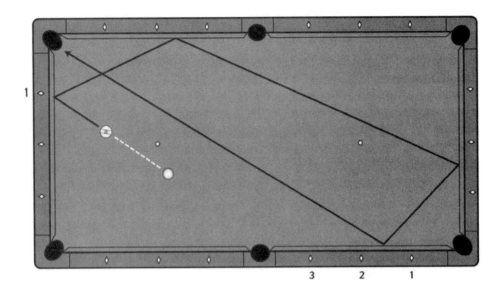

THE FOUR RAIL BANK SHOT

This is another one of those shots that is used when playing one pocket. Normally it is used when the direct path to the pocket is blocked and there is a cluster of balls to block your opponent if the shot is missed. Here the object ball is directly in line with the side rail diamond #3 and the end rail diamond #1. Shoot the bank with a forceful stroke and a dead center cue ball hit. The object ball will go four rails into the corner pocket. Notice how the rebound angles off cushions 3 & 4 are much wider than the rebound angles off the first two cushions. Again this is caused by the english picked up by the object ball from the cushions. Practice this shot using a striped object ball. Notice how the object ball is spinning as it comes up the table. It will actually still be spinning as it drops into the hole.

Chapter Six
Combinations

Combinations are extremely difficult shots. First, the cue ball must strike an object ball at an exact point. Then, this object ball must strike the next ball at another exact point. And finally, this object ball must find the opening to the pocket. Any slight error is compounded by each contact of the balls. An error in calculation or missed contact point on the first ball will greatly effect the accuracy of the shot. This is why most professionals almost always avoid combinations.

While combinations are very difficult, they are not impossible. There are many theories or systems that can greatly improve your combination pocketing ability. In the following illustrations, I will discuss 5 of these systems. These systems are:

1) In line cue stick theory

2) Ghost ball theory

3) 1 & 1/8 inch theory

4) Spot on the rail/cushion theory

5) Throw theory

Even though these systems are very helpful in improving your combination pocketing percentage, I suggest you ask yourself the following questions first before you shoot a combination:

1) If you miss, will it probably result in a lost game? Many missed "combos" will leave the ball in the "jaws" of the pocket (especially the 9 ball).

2) Can you play a better safety? Remember what you learned in Chapter 3 how easy it is to play a safety by simply hiding the cue ball behind another object ball.

3) Do you have CONFIDENCE in your ability to execute this shot? Some days you DO and some days you DON'T.

4) Is it easier to run the table? This usually occurs in a nine ball game when you have ball in hand and are contemplating a combination shot on the nine ball.

So as you can see, it is usually better to avoid most combination shots. Also most combinations that are made are fairly close to the pocket with the effected balls close to
each other. Rarely will you see a combination attempted from the middle of the table
especially if there is any measurable distance separating the balls. Once you have
decided to shoot the "combo", the following two things must be executed perfectly:

**1) The calculation and measurement of the contact point on the first ball
must be perfect.**

**2) This point then must be contacted by the cue ball using a slightly above
perpendicular center ball hit with a loose medium force stroke. I cannot
emphasize enough the importance of this hit on all combination shots.
The high english on the cue ball will cause less slide and a cleaner separation with the object ball allowing for greater accuracy. Do not add
any side spin (some exceptions) as "throw" and "squirt" (Chapter 13)
must be avoided to ensure accurac**y.

Learn the following systems and principles. Practice them and find the ones that work
best for you. But always remember what I said earlier. **"Avoid combinations whenever possible."**

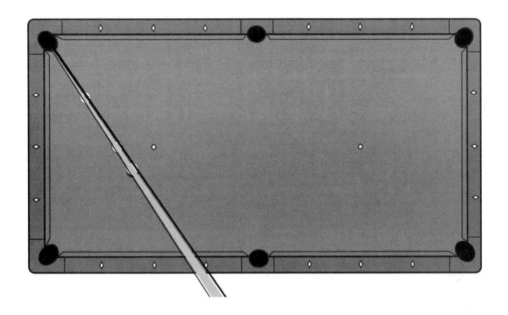

THE CUE STICK IN LINE THEORY

This is the easiest of all the combination theories. Use this principle when the two object balls are directly in line with the pocket and you have ball-in-hand. Simply place the tip of the cue stick at the center of the pocket and extend it over the two object balls. Now place the cue ball about 2-4 inches behind the first object ball and directly underneath the cue stick. Hold the cue stick above the centers of all three balls and reaffirm the cue tip is pointing to the center of the pocket. If not, pick up the cue ball and start the alignment process over again. Once all three balls are directly in line with the center of the pocket, you can aim the cue ball at any of the 3 reference points-the center of the first object ball, the center of the second object ball, or the center of the pocket.

Shoot this shot with a dead center ball hit on the cue ball and a moderate stroke. Do not "baby" this shot as a missed combination with a soft hit usually leaves the object ball close to the pocket for an even easier combination for your opponent. Also be sure to place the cue ball close to the first object ball. The greater the distance the cue ball is from the first object ball, the more it increases the margin for error. I have even seen some of the pro players line this shot up with the cue ball 1-2 feet from the first object ball. Only their uncanny accuracy saves them from missing this shot. Unless you are a professional player, keep the cue ball close to the first object ball on all ball-in-hand combination situations.

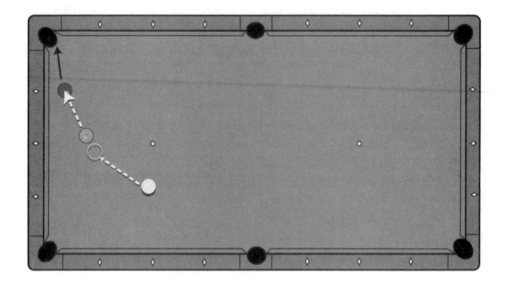

THE GHOST BALL COMBINATION THEORY

Here you imagine where the cue ball must strike the first object ball to pocket the second object ball. Then it is as simple as replacing the "ghost" cue ball with the actual cue ball. Again use a moderate stroke and an above center ball hit on the cue ball. If the cue ball contacts the first object ball where you imagined the "ghost" cue ball would contact this ball, the second object ball will be pocketed into the corner pocket.

Practice this ghost ball combination theory. Start with the balls close together and close to the pocket. As your pocketing skills improve, increase the distance between the object balls and the distance to the pocket. Notice how your accuracy erodes as the distance between the object balls and the pocket increases. Also the greater the angle, the more difficult the combination becomes. So as the distance to the pocket increases, the distance between the object balls increases, and as the angle increases, the more difficult the combination becomes. A safety is usually the more prudent shot to play rather than attempt a difficult combination.

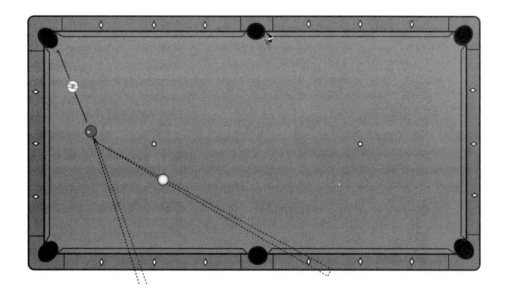

THE 1 & 1/8 INCH COMBINATION THEORY

Here you first line up the shot with the cue stick directly behind the first object ball and the tip on the cloth directly under the edge of the ball. So if you were allowed to shoot the first object ball into the second object ball you would be in line to pocket the object ball into the center of the pocket. Now pull the cue stick back 1 & 1/8 inches still leaving the tip of the cue stick on the cloth. Remember the balls are 2 1/4 inches in diameter. So from the center of the cue ball to the edge is 1 & 1/8 inches. The spot (x) on the cloth where the tip is now represents the center of the cue ball when it would come in contact to the object ball to pocket the second object ball. Now rotate the butt end of the cue directly over the cue ball.

Be sure not to move the tip away from the spot on the cloth. You have now established the line the cue ball must travel to make the combination. Pull the cue stick back over the cue ball keeping it directly on the shooting line. Aim along this line to the spot (X) on the cloth in front of the object ball. As always, use a moderate stroke and a high english only hit on the cue ball.

125

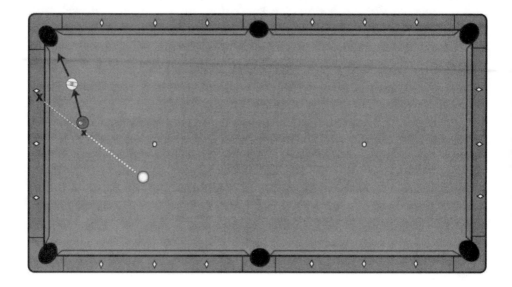

THE SPOT ON THE RAIL/CUSHION COMBINATION THEORY

Here you find your contact point by either the ghost ball theory or the 1 & 1/8 inch ball theory. Now you extend the cue stick from the center of the cue ball and center of the ghost ball (or the 1& 1/8 inch spot on the cloth) to the rail. The spot (x) where the cue tip contacts the rail is the aiming point to pocket the combination. Visually (it is illegal to physically mark this spot), mark this spot on the cushion or rail. Usually there is some sort of a reference point such as a rail diamond or possibly writing on the cloth on the bottom side of the rail cushion. Aim directly at this spot with an above center ball hit and a moderate stroke.

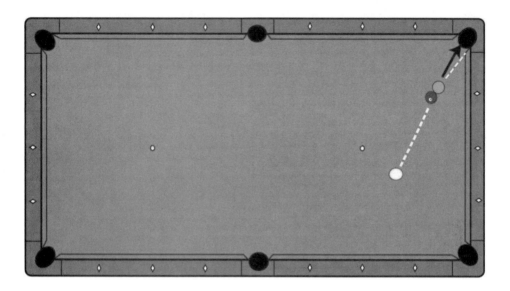

THE FROZEN BALL COMBINATION

The above illustration shows a combination of two object balls touching each other and aimed just outside the pocket. Your initial reaction is the combination cannot be made. In order to make the combination, the second object ball path must be altered. This can be accomplished by hitting the first object ball with the cue ball slightly off to the right side with about a 3/4 ball hit. This will cause the first object ball to spin slightly to the right. The 3/4 ball hit will give you the maximum amount of spin. Aiming more outside the first object will reduce the amount of spin. This slight spin will "throw" the second object ball slightly to the left towards the pocket away from its original line. The hit on these "throw" combinations requires a much softer hit than on the other types of combinations. A softer hit on the first object ball will give you the maximum amount of throw. A harder hit will minimize the thrown. More will be discussed on this concept in chapter 13.

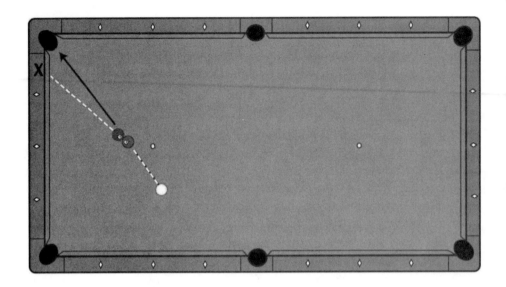

THROW WITH ENGLISH COMBINATIONS

The above two balls are frozen together and aimed at about the 1/2 diamond mark on the end rail. If you aim the cue ball at the 3/4 object ball point on the left, the second object ball path will be altered only to about the 1/4 diamond mark. You must figure a way to further widen the path of the second object ball. Applying right english to the cue ball will transfer left spin to the first object ball. Hitting the first object ball on the left will also cause it to spin to the left. Both of these two actions work synergistically together to enhance the spin on the first object ball. The added spin will further widen the path of the second object ball. Again, use a soft hit on the cue ball, and the path of the second object ball will be altered towards the pocket.

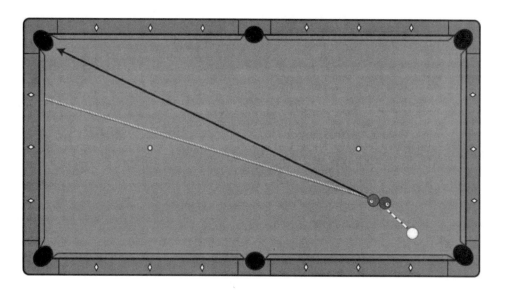

MAXIMUM ENGLISH FROZEN THROW COMBINATION

The above illustration shows a frozen combination aimed to the first diamond on the end rail. Again, by applying right spin to the cue ball and contacting the first object ball on the left at about the 3/4 ball point, the second object ball will be "thrown" into the corner pocket. This is about the maximum amount the path of a frozen ball can be altered. Cleanliness of the balls and cloth and the humidity in the room will determine the maximum amount of throw on a frozen combination.

Chapter Seven
Caroms

Caroms are very similar to combinations. In fact, I will illustrate 3 of the same systems that you were shown in Chapter 6 on combinations. The difference between the two is that on a combination shot, you are trying to pocket the object ball with another object ball and on a carom shot, you are trying to pocket the object ball with the cue ball after it has struck another object ball. There are 4 basic types of caroms:

1) **Dead carom.**

2) **Frozen carom.**

3) **Non-frozen carom.**

4) **Throw carom.**

The following three systems or theories will illustrate how to take the guesswork out of figuring out a carom shot:

1) **Ghost ball theory.**

2) **1 & 1/8 inch theory.**

3) **Spot on the rail/cushion theory.**

But before I get into the discussion and illustration of these shots, you must first understand the "tangent line". When the cue ball strikes an object ball at an angle, it will rebound away along the tangent line. This imaginary line is formed perpendicular to the exact point of contact of the two balls. So if you could draw a line directly through the centers of the cue ball and the object ball at the instant of contact, the tangent line rebound path of the cue ball would be perpendicular (90 degrees angle) to the line through the centers of these balls (Fig. 1). The understanding and calculation of this line is necessary for proper execution of these carom shots. Also this line becomes even more important to understand in Chapter 11 with the discussion of position play. This rebound line can also be changed by applying english (high or low) to the cue ball. Side english with not alter the tangent line. The following pages will illustrate these principles and theories. Practice these examples until you get a "feel" for these shots. It is more important to understand the "how" and "why" in this chapter than to spend a lot of time practicing these carom shots.

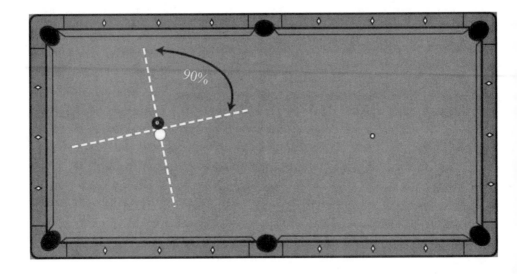

THE TANGENT LINE (FIG #1)

The above illustration shows the cue ball striking the object ball at the exact point of contact. Here the cue ball is contacting the object ball dead center or straight on. By drawing a line through the centers of the two balls and then another line perpendicular to this line through the contact point, a 90 degree angle would be formed. If the cue ball could rebound away from the object ball, it would follow the 90 degree angle line. But since the object ball is struck dead center, all the energy of the cue ball is transferred to the object ball straight ahead. The cue ball will therefore stop dead at the contact point. If high or low english is applied to the cue ball, the cue ball will either follow or draw back in a straight line.

However, if the object ball is contacted at an angle, the cue ball will rebound at the opposite angle and follow the tangent line. So if the object ball is hit at a 30 degree angle, the cue ball will rebound at a 60 degree angle (90-30=60). This simple formula will work for virtually all ball collisions. The rebound angle or tangent line can be altered by applying various types of english to the cue ball. But for most caroms, always use a dead center cue ball hit so the cue ball will rebound along the natural predictable tangent line angle.

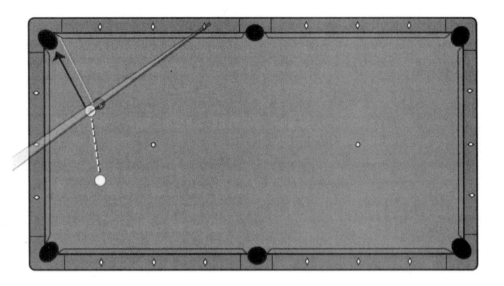

THE FROZEN DEAD CAROM

The above frozen ball carom is dead into the corner pocket. You first determine this by placing the cue stick above the two object balls and directly through their centers. Now draw an imaginary line perpendicular (90 degrees) to the cue stick directly through the junction of the two object balls. In the above illustration, that line is aimed at the edge of the pocket. If the cue ball is aimed at the first object ball head on, the first object ball will "carom" off the second object ball and follow the path parallel to the imaginary tangent line. Since the center of the object ball is 1 & 1/8 inches from the imaginary path line, the object ball path will be directly into the center of the pocket. Use a medium stroke and a dead center cue ball hit.

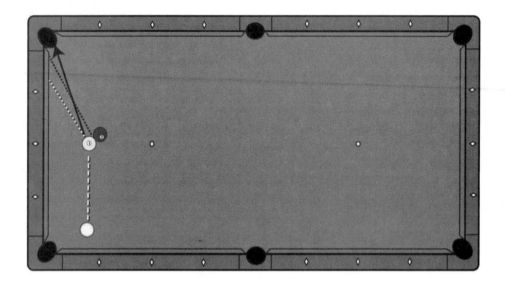

THE SHORT FROZEN CAROM

Again, you have two balls frozen together. By placing the cue stick above the two balls and through their centers, you can draw an imaginary line perpendicular to the stick from the junction of the two balls. This time that line is aimed at the bottom edge of the pocket. Since the first object ball will carom off the second object ball and follow a path 1& 1/8 inches parallel to this line, the object ball will head towards the end rail cushion with a center ball hit on the cue ball. You must figure out a way to alter the path of the object ball to get it to go wide of the tangent rebound line towards the pocket. This can be done by applying low english on the cue ball. This low cue ball spin will transfer follow spin to the first object ball causing the object ball to go wide of the tangent line towards the pocket.

Notice how the object ball path to the pocket traverses across the natural tangent line path. These shots are shot softly with about 1-2 tips of low english for maximum effect. These shots become more difficult as the distance between the first object ball and the cue ball increases. The friction of the cloth removes much of the draw spin as the cue ball travels 5-6 feet before striking the first object ball.

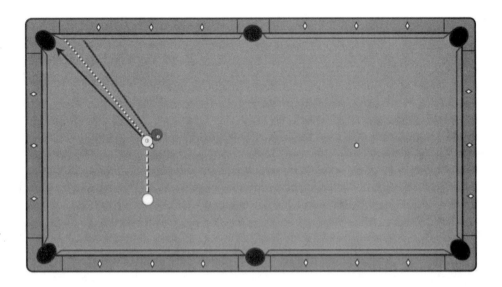

THE WIDE FROZEN CAROM

This time your tangent line is aimed slightly wide of the pocket. A center ball hit on the cue ball and a full hit on the object ball will cause the contacted object ball to carom off the second object ball into the side rail cushion. By applying high or follow english to the cue ball, you can impart low english to the first object ball. This will cause the first object ball path to be altered short of the tangent line towards the pocket. Again, use a soft hit on the cue ball with about 1-2 tips of high english for maximum effect. I suggest you practice all three frozen ball carom examples. Use the white reinforcement donuts for a consistent set up. Alter the cue ball speed and the amount and type of english applied until you are comfortable with a consistent desired result.

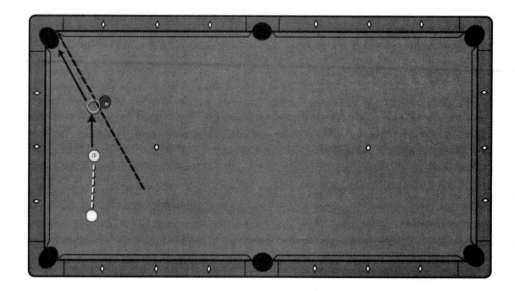

THE GHOST BALL CAROM THEORY

This theory is virtually the same as the ghost ball combination theory. First, place the cue stick tip at the edge of the pocket and directly over the edge of the object ball to be used as the carom ball. Now imagine another object ball touching the carom ball to be used and perpendicular to the line to the pocket. You now have formed and visualized a frozen dead carom shot in your head. All you have to do now is to hit the first object ball to the spot of the "ghost" object ball and the first object ball will carom off the user ball into the corner pocket. Use a high english hit on the cue ball to reduce slide and cause a cleaner separation of the balls. Use only a soft stroke to ensure accuracy. Most advanced players use this carom theory.

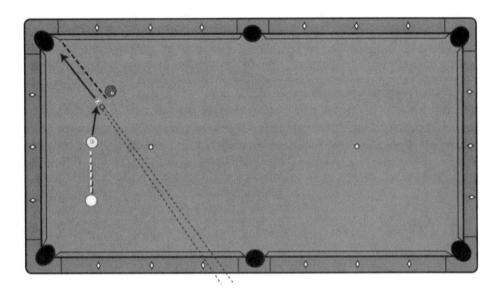

THE 1 & 1/8 INCH CAROM BALL THEORY

Again, this theory is the same as the 1 & 1/8 inch combination theory. First, place the cue stick over the edge of the user carom ball and the cue tip at the edge of the pocket. Now slide the cue tip back along the cloth keeping it on this tangent line. Once you get to the spot directly across from the user carom ball and perpendicular to the original line, roll the cue stick tip until it is 1 & 1/8 inches away from the edge of the user carom ball. This spot (x) is where you want the center of the first object ball to go. Rotate the butt end of the stick over the first object ball being careful not to move the tip away from the calculated spot on the cloth. You now have the line the first object ball must travel to the calculated spot to carom off the user object ball into the corner pocket. Use a smooth slow to moderate stroke and a high english cue ball hit.

This theory is very similar to the ghost ball theory but some players prefer to shoot the object ball to a "spot" while other players can visualize where they want the object ball to contact the user ball.

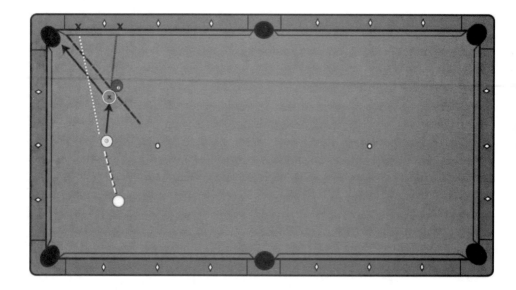

THE SPOT ON THE RAIL/CUSHION CAROM THEORY

At first, the above diagram looks very confusing. This is just like the previous carom theories, but one or two more steps are added. As always, first find the tangent line from the edge of the pocket to the edge of the user carom ball. Now use either the ghost ball theory or the 1 & 1/8 inch ball theory (x) to obtain the spot where you want the carom ball to rebound off the user ball that is perpendicular to the tangent line. Now instead of aiming to this spot, extend the line from the carom ball to this spot and beyond to the rail/cushion. Visually (it is illegal to physically mark the spot), mark this spot and aim the carom ball at this spot on the rail. Or you can determine the spot on the carom ball that the cue ball must hit and extend this line to the rail. Again, visually mark this spot on the rail and aim the cue ball directly at this spot.

So both of these two variations depend on aiming the carom ball at a spot on the rail/cushion or aiming the cue ball at a spot on the rail/cushion. Some of the professionals think they can be more accurate by aiming at a spot farther in the distance. Again, shoot these shots with a slow to moderate stroke and an above center cue ball hit.

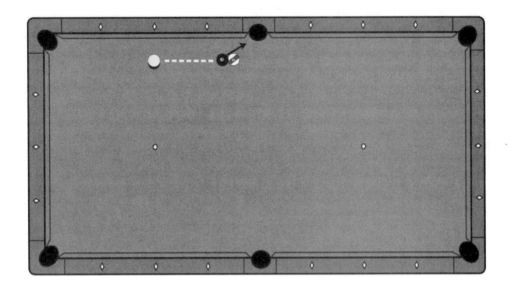

THE FROZEN BALL CAROM SHOT

Assume you are playing eight ball and you have run all the solids and are left with the eight ball up against one of your opponent's striped balls as illustrated. At first glance, playing a safety may be the prudent shot. But by understanding the frozen ball carom theories, you can actually make the eight ball into the side pocket. By applying about 1-2 tips of low english to the cue ball and using a fairly crisp stroke, the back spin on the cue ball will transfer some forward spin to the eight ball. This will cause the eight ball to move straight forward if it is contacted dead on by the cue ball. But the eight ball also needs to move towards the left if it is to be made into the side pocket. This can be accomplished a couple of ways.

First is to strike the object ball straight on but use low right english on the cue ball. This will transfer left spin to the eight ball. The left spin on the eight ball will alter the course of the nine ball to the right, and the eight ball will carom off the nine ball and spin towards the side pocket. The second way is to shoot this shot slightly off center to the right of the eight ball. Use only low english on the cue ball, and the off center hit on the eight ball will push the eight ball towards the side pocket. Practice both of these shots and see which one works best for you.

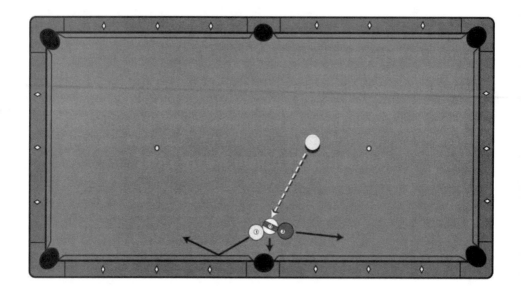

THE MULTIPLE BALL FROZEN CAROM SHOT

This is another one of those eight ball situations where your striped ball is frozen against two of your opponents' solid balls. You probably know the striped ball will go into the side pocket. You just don't know how to do it. But by understanding the carom and tangent line principles, it is really easy to figure. I like to work these shots out backwards. First, determine the solid ball the striped ball must carom off to go into the side pocket. Placing the cue stick over the junction of the striped ball and the solid ball left of the pocket and perpendicular to their centers will give you a tangent line to the cushion above the pocket. On the other hand, placing the cue stick over the junction of the striped ball and the solid ball right of the pocket and perpendicular to their centers will give you a tangent line to the pocket.

So now you have determined that the solid ball right of the pocket is your carom user ball. In order for the striped ball to carom off this solid ball into the side pocket, the other solid ball left of the pocket must get out of the way first. The side on which the eleven ball is contacted by the cue ball determines which solid ball will move first. By contacting the eleven ball on the left as illustrated, the solid ball left of the pocket will move first, and the striped ball will carom off the solid ball right of the pocket into the side pocket. This process occurs in milliseconds and cannot be detected by the naked eye. Try contacting the eleven ball right of center by the cue ball and notice how the eleven ball goes into the cushion right of the pocket. Use a dead center or slightly above center cue ball hit and a moderate stroke.

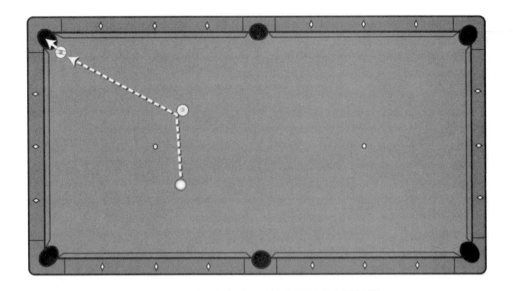

THE MOST COMMON CAROM SHOT

Cue ball caroms are the easiest and most common type of caroms played. They occur quite often when playing nine ball. In almost all cases, the object ball to be made is very close to a pocket. The above illustration comes up fairly often. Your opponent has broken the nine ball rack without pocketing a ball and almost making the nine ball into the corner pocket. Fortunately for you, you have a carom shot using the cue ball off the one ball into the nine ball. As before, point the cue stick tip at the outside edge of the nine ball and rotate the cue stick over the edge of the one ball to be contacted by the cue ball. This is the tangent line towards the nine ball. Now determine where you want the one ball to be contacted by the cue ball by any of the previously discussed theories. Shoot the shot with a slightly above dead center cue ball hit and a moderate stroke.

The negative of these cue ball carom shots towards an object ball in front of a pocket is that the cue ball can also follow the object ball into the pocket. So instead of determining the tangent line from the user ball to the edge of the nine ball, it may be better to move the tangent line slightly up the side rail cushion. Now the cue ball will carom off the one ball slightly wide of the pocket into the side rail cushion and rebound off the cushion pocketing the nine ball. This eliminates the possibility of a scratch.

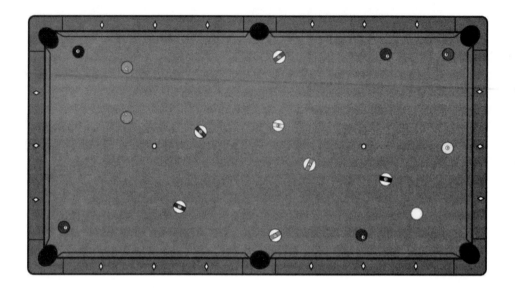

THE BEST CAROM BALL DRILL

This is the best drill to develop your carom skills. Randomly, place all fifteen balls around the table. Place several of the balls close to the pockets. Now take cue ball-in-hand and try to carom the cue ball off any object ball and pocket the cue ball. After each shot is made or missed, take cue ball-in-hand and continue on with the drill. Once you get a good feel for the cue ball caroms and are pocketing the cue ball or at least getting it very close to the pocket, carom the cue ball off any object ball and try to make another object ball. Start with the object balls that are close to a pocket. Don't be surprised if it takes 100-200 shots just to clear one rack of balls off the table. After your skills improve, don't take cue ball in hand after each shot. Shoot from wherever the cue ball lands. This makes the drill considerably more difficult.

Improving your carom skills will take hours and hours of practice. It is a very difficult part of the game and can become very frustrating during practice sessions. I always suggest putting a time limit or rack limit on these practice drills. Before you start these practice sessions, limit yourself to one hour or 1-3 racks. Your concentration will eventually begin to wander over an hour at this drill and your frustration will rise. Remember, this is a very difficult part of the game.

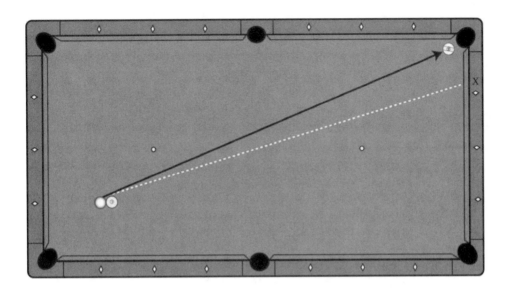

THE FROZEN CUE BALL DOUBLE DIVISION CAROM SHOT

Here you have broken the nine ball rack and made a ball but the cue ball has ended up frozen to the one ball. To make matters worse, you have left the nine ball in the "jaws" of the corner pocket. You can't throw the one ball into the corner pocket and you can't knock the nine ball away from the pocket. Your situation seems very bleak. But actually you can carom the cue ball off the one ball pocketing the nine ball into the corner pocket. Professional pool and billiard instructor, Wayne Norcross, taught me this simple cue ball frozen to the object ball theory shot. I call this the double division carom shot. First measure the distance on the rail between where the two frozen balls are aimed and the intended object ball. In the above example, the two frozen balls are aimed at the third diamond on the end rail.

Since the nine ball is in front of the corner pocket, the distance between the nine ball and the two frozen balls aiming point is 3 diamonds. Now simply divide this number in half (3 divided by 2 = 1 & 1/2). Now divide this number in half again (1 & 1/2 divided by 2 = 3/4). You have now calculated the aiming spot on the cushion where you must aim the cue ball for it to carom off the one ball towards the nine ball in front of the corner pocket. Aim at the 3/4 diamond mark on the end rail cushion and use a soft center cue ball hit. The cue ball will carom off the one ball and continue down the table pocketing the nine ball into the corner pocket. The key to this shot is that the cue ball must be frozen to the object ball. Also side spin must not be applied to the cue ball.

143

Chapter Eight
The Nine Ball Break

As you become a better player, a good break is what is needed to play "run out" pool. Most of the discussion here will be regarding the nine ball break. When the professionals play, usually the one breaking the best wins. If they can pocket 1-2 balls, position the cue ball in the center of the table, and have a shot on the next ball, they almost always run out. There are many factors that contribute to a good break. The most important aspect of the break is a solid hit on the head ball and the least important is power. Do I hear some disagreement here? Have you ever seen a 150 pound professional baseball player hit a home run over the center field fence 400 feet away. Or a slightly built golfer drive a golf ball 300 yards. They do not accomplish these feats with miraculous power, but use bat or club head speed to propel the ball. The same analogy can be used for the nine ball break. The goal is to propel the cue ball as fast as possible into the head ball as solid as possible. When this is done, you will hear a very distinctive sound and watch heads turn. The following will cover each of the steps necessary to accomplish the "POWER BREAK".

THE SET UP

Since you will be using almost your maximum speed, it is imperative the head ball is hit solid. Therefore, your body position is extremely important. Approach this shot no differently than any other shot-from several feet behind the table. Your stance should be slightly closer to the table, narrower, a little more sideways, and higher than your normal shot. This will eliminate the natural barriers for maximum follow through.

THE BRIDGE

While I have seen many great "breakers" use a very long bridge, usually a shorter bridge is better. The shorter bridge does three things. First, it improves accuracy. Second, it helps keep the cue tip along the perpendicular centerline axis of the cue ball. Any sideways movement of the back hand will be reflected less at the tip of the cue stick with a shorter bridge. This fulcrum theory will be discussed more in Chapter 13. And finally, a shorter bridge allows for a longer follow through necessary for a good break.

BRIDGE ARM

The bridge arm should be relaxed and bent. If this arm is straight or locked, it will prevent needed forward body movement to finish the stroke.

THE GRIP

The grip should be as loose as possible. It is only there to hold the cue from dropping to the floor and with enough pressure to allow your bicep and body to propel the cue forward. Also your hand should be positioned a little more forward to compensate for the shorter bridge and a slightly higher stance and to reduce any pendulum action of the cue stick.

THE WRIST

This is a major source of the cue stick speed. This increased speed comes from the "snap" action of the wrist. When I was a kid, we used to play a game called mumbletypeg. This game involved flipping a knife and sticking it in the ground at a specific spot. It required a loose, snap action wrist movement. This same movement is required for the break. Phil Capelle in his *Play Your Best Nine Ball* book talks about Francisco Bustamante having one of the "supplest wrists in pool". Francisco is not a big guy, but he can really break a nine ball rack.

THE LOWER BODY

This is where the baseball players and golfers really get their power. To get that distinctive sound of a great break, the lower body is needed to add to what the arm and wrist is accomplishing. Getting your hips and legs to begin accelerating forward just before your cue starts forward is the only power source of the break. Now you have the added weight of your body moving forward behind the cue stick.

THE CUE BALL

The break is one of the few shots where you are looking at the cue ball on tip contact. If you have set up properly, you should be in line to hit the head ball solid. Since you are using your maximum controllable speed, the cue ball must be hit dead center or slightly below center. Any left or right english will cause the cue ball to "squirt" away from a solid hit. Basically any hit away from dead center will result in loss of energy and speed. I am sure you have seen some very good "breakers" have their tip on the cloth during their warm up strokes. This is done for 3 reasons:

1) They can see the reflection of their cue tip on the base of the cue ball to be sure they are perfectly perpendicularly centered.

2) As they accelerate to the cue ball, the natural tendency is for the cue tip to rise.

3) They also purposely bring the cue tip straight up on the final stroke.

THE FOLLOW THROUGH

This is the last but not the least aspect of the power break. If everything is done correctly, your whole body is moving forward with your cue stick following through and extending beyond mid-table and your back foot leaving the floor. Johnny Archer has the best follow through in professional pool. He has even fouled because his cue tip has gone so far that it has contacted one of the racked balls.

Now you know that producing a good break requires lots of knowledge and execution. My suggestion is to not try all of these things at once. Start with a short bridge and no body movement. If you are getting consistently good solid hits, add a little more follow through. If you are consistent here, add the body movement. The break shot is really a timing exercise. The body starts forward, then the cue starts forward, then the wrist snaps, then the cue stick follows through with the back foot leaving the floor. Then you hear that distinctive sound and watch the heads turn.

I would also like to clear up a speed misconception. Many players think they break the balls at some unheard of speed. Truth is most professionals break around 25 MPH. Very seldom do they ever break the 30 MPH barrier.

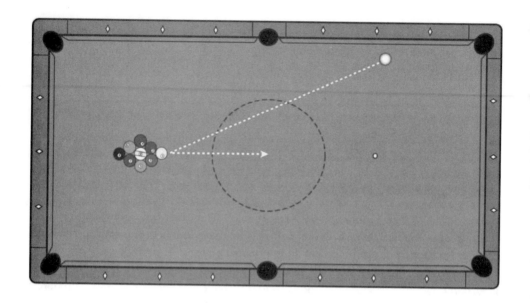

THE KEY TO THE 9 BALL BREAK

The key to the power 9 ball break is a solid hit on the one ball and control of the cue ball towards the middle of the table. If the one ball is hit solid, a slightly below center cue ball hit will draw the cue back towards the middle of the table. The best action on the balls usually occurs when the breaker is positioned bridging off the rail with the cue ball at about the head string and 2-3 inches in from the cushion. From this position, the breaker is hitting slightly down on the cue ball causing it to go airborne, as it heads towards the one ball. Some of the best 9 ball breakers have almost perfected hitting the one ball on the "fly", reducing any loss of speed the friction of the felt would have removed from the cue ball. Unfortunately, 90% of all pool players are unable to master this break from that position. Most players breaking from this position fail to contact the one ball fully, scratch, or cause the cue ball to leave the table.

I always suggest starting in the middle of the table and use about 75% of your speed. As your breaks and cue ball control improve, begin to move more to the side. Only move to the side as far as the table will allow your bridge hand to remain on the cloth. Once you are breaking well and controlling the cue ball from the side, move your speed up to about 85-90%.

Any more than this usually results in loss of accuracy. Remember Rule #1 from *The Winning Rules For 9 Ball* as it is probably the most important rule for good 9 ball players.

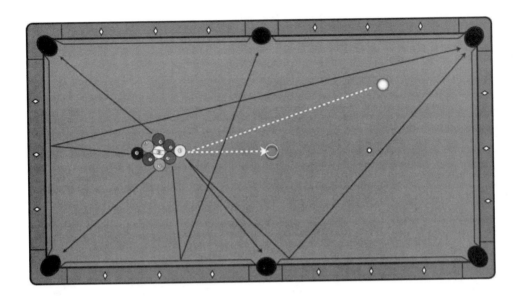

THE 9 BALL BREAK-MAKING BALLS

The above diagram indicates the paths of the most common balls that are pocketed on the nine ball break. Remember this diagram when you are racking if you are playing a lesser opponent and you are giving up a ball or two. If you are giving up the eight ball, most players prefer to put it behind the one ball. But as you can see, the breaker will break from the opposite side that the eight ball is on to try and bank it into the side pocket. A lot of players prefer to put the "given up" balls directly behind the 9 ball. While there is no consistency where these two balls go, they seem to get a lot of action from the rest of the balls from the rack. This is a good spot to "hide" these "given up" balls for a player with a weak break.

As I mentioned earlier, making the cue ball on the break is one ball you do not want to pocket. The majority of all scratches on the break are caused by the cue ball crossing the face of the one ball. When this happens, very little energy is transferred from the cue ball to the one ball and the remaining cue ball energy propels the cue ball around the table looking for a pocket. I am sure you may have noticed that many of the professional players have really "backed off" on their break. With their perfect conditions (perfect rack each time, new cloth, new, balls, etc.), they are able to make the corner ball each time while drawing the cue ball to the side rail cushion and rebounding towards the middle of the table. They do this by hitting the one ball slightly off center towards the same side rail with low english. Unfortunately, most players do not get these ideal conditions.

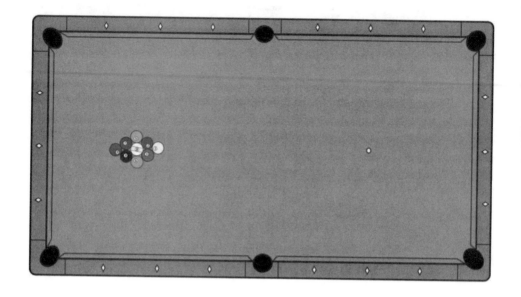

THE RACK FOR LESSER PLAYERS

There are several legal things you can do to give you an advantage when racking the balls for your opponent's break. First of all, you should try to rack the balls as tightly as possible. All the balls should be touching each other. Unfortunately, the equipment most of us play with is not as precise as what the professionals use. The triangle may be warped, the balls may be of different sizes, the cloth may have ball indentations, and the slate may even have some indentations especially around the spot. All of these conditions contribute to a less than perfect rack. Always try to get as many of the balls touching each other as possible, especially the first three balls. This will keep the game as fair as possible with your opponent. And always have the two back balls touching the nine ball. Any gap between these balls and the nine ball can send the nine ball toward the corner pocket.

When you are playing a lesser player that normally will not run out or a player with a weak break, the above illustration shows a ball racking order that may give you a slight advantage. The idea here is to cluster the low numbered balls and the high numbered balls together so that they remain close together after the break. This way you will not have to move the cue ball as far as you go from ball to ball during your run out.

THE RACK FOR BETTER PLAYERS

The above illustrated ball racking order works exactly opposite when racking for a good player that can run out. This order will separate the low and high number balls from each other as much as possible, making your opponents move the cue ball greater distances as they go from ball to ball. Hopefully what will happen is your opponents will run several balls as they struggle for position before finally missing a shot. Now you have an open table with only several balls left. If your opponents are consistently making the one ball on the break and getting position on the two ball, try moving the two ball to the back of the rack. The cluster of balls will many times keep the two ball close to the end rail. Also, always try to rack the one ball directly on the spot. Any placement of the rack more towards the end rail increases the chances of one of the corner balls going into the corner pocket. And finally never let your opponents rack for themselves. If your opponent has already racked the balls before the lag or coin flip and they win the break, be sure to re-rack the balls. They may have left a gap behind the nine ball to increase their chances of making the nine ball on the break.

Practicing the break can become very tedious. There is a company called BreakRAK L.L.C. that has developed an artificial racking system that simulates an actual nine ball rack. This will allow you to practice your break fundamentals and cue ball control without racking the balls each time. They can be reached on the internet at www.breakrak.com.

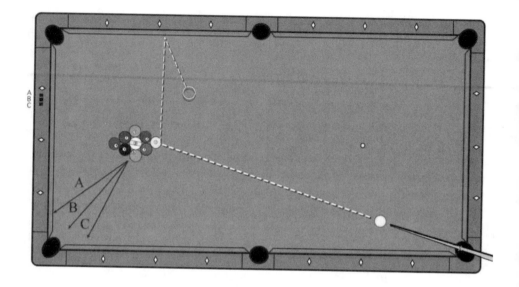

THE "SOFT" NINE BALL BREAK

Some of the "pool schools" and pool instructors have been teaching several types of softer breaks for nine ball for the past several years. These breaking techniques rely more on pocketing a specific ball and controlling the cue ball than just a powerful smattering of the balls. If after everything you have learned and practiced in this chapter has still not given you a good break, you may want to experiment with this one illustrated above. This softer break keeps all the balls at one end of the table. You must have a good command of the cue ball and be able to position "whitey" very accurately because all the object balls are in close proximity to each other. This is an excellent break to use against weaker players as they usually will hook themselves behind an obstructer sometime during their turn at the table. Also if you scratch a lot on the break, this softer break virtually eliminates that possibility. And although this break results many times in less run outs, it can result in the breaker having better command of the table. They will pocket several balls and then play a nice roll up safety (Chapter #3) behind an obstructer ball forcing their opponents to constantly kick at balls.

The set up on this break is very simple. But you must practice it before you actually try it in a match. Place the cue ball on the head string directly in line with the center of the back corner pocket and the one ball. Place three chalks on the far end rail beginning at the edge of the first diamond. Aiming at chalk "A" will move the corner ball towards the end rail. Aiming at chalk "B" will move it towards the corner pocket. And aiming at chalk "C" will move the corner ball towards the side rail. Use a soft stroke but be sure to have 4 balls contact the cushions for a legal nine ball break.

Chapter Nine
The Masse Shot

Sometimes when you are blocked on a shot, the only way or the best way may be to "bend" or masse the cue ball around the obstructer ball. This shot requires a special feel. This feel can only be obtained with practice. Unfortunately, practicing these shots plays havoc with the equipment. My suggestion here is to ask the pool hall proprietor where you play when he is going to recover a table. Then go in a day or so before the table is recovered and practice these illustrated masse shots. Be sure also to get his permission.

The masse shot is performed by hitting at a down angle on the cue ball and towards one side. This initially will cause the cue ball to "squirt" out a little while the english will take hold several inches or feet down the table bringing it back to the original line or more. The more the cue stick is elevated at the butt, the more the cue ball will bend. The harder it is hit, the more distance it will travel before it bends. The masse shot is performed best with a soft cue tip and a stiff shaft. Use a very loose (even a 2 finger) grip with a good slow follow through stroke. This loose slow rolling stroke on the cue ball is best for control of the bend and prevents the cue ball from leaving the table surface. Your cue tip should actually strike the cloth and proceed for 4-8 inches. This is why pool hall proprietors do not like this shot. For short partially blocked shots, just elevate the butt of the cue stick slightly and use low side english. For fully blocked balls, elevate the butt of the cue stick more, aiming down on the side of the cue ball and aiming about one ball width outside the obstructer ball.

Practice the following illustrations. Just practice them enough to get a feel for them. These shots are too tough on the equipment for much practice. It is more important to understand the why and how. Then when you are in a game situation, you will understand how to execute the shot. These almost always are last resort shots.

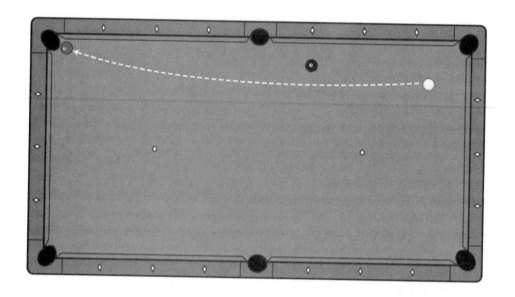

THE MASSE SHOT

Here your shot at the ball in front of the corner pocket is partially blocked by another obstructer ball. The goal is to alter the path of the cue ball so it misses the obstructer ball but goes towards the ball in front of the corner pocket. This can be done by aiming at the left edge of the blocker ball with the right edge of the cue ball and shooting down on the cue ball with the butt end of the stick slightly elevated. Since you want the cue ball to curve to the right, apply low right hand english on the cue ball. The cue ball will first "squirt" a little to the left away from the obstructer ball, and then the low right spin will grab the cloth as it "hops" along the bed, causing the cue ball to curve towards the intended object ball.

For shots with the blocker ball less than 3 feet away from the cue ball, use low right english with the butt end of the cue slightly elevated. For shots greater than 4 feet, elevate the butt end of the cue stick more and aim only on the right side of the cue ball. Use a little more forceful stroke. Both the more forceful stroke and higher angle of the cue stick will cause the cue ball to "squirt" more away from the shooting line and then the english will bend the cue ball back towards its intended target. Always use a very loose slow to moderate stroke and good follow through. The cue tip should slide across the cloth for several inches. And like the break shot, always look at the cue ball on the final stroke.

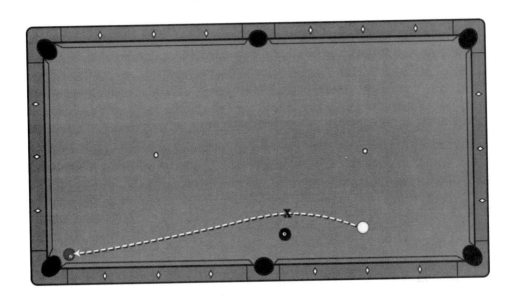

THE MORE EXTREME MASSE SHOT

Here the path to the corner object ball is completely blocked. This time, aim at a spot on the cloth about 1 & 1/2 balls width outside the obstructer ball. One of the keys to this shot is to ignore the object balls, and do your set up on the cue ball aiming at this spot on the cloth. Be sure to start your set up by approaching the table from several feet, keeping the cue ball in line with this spot on the cloth. Another way to keep you inline on this shot is to place the cue tip on this spot outside the obstructer ball and drag it back along the cloth and directly over the cue ball. Now you will have the cue stick on the proper line to the target as you elevate the butt end. Elevate the butt end of the stick about 2 feet above the table and shoot down on the cue ball. This time the cue ball will need to curve to the left so aim at the left side of the cue ball. Again, use a slow to moderate smooth stroke and a good follow through. The cue ball will "squirt" slightly more to the right, but the left spin will bring it around the obstructer ball towards the ball in front of the corner pocket. As in all masse shots, be sure to be look- ing at the cue ball on the final stroke.

A must for all masse shots is to be sure you miss the obstructer ball. Hitting this ball gives you no chance of a legal shot. Even if you do not bend the cue ball enough around the obstructer ball, many times the cue ball will spin off the cushion into the intended object ball preventing giving up ball-in-hand.

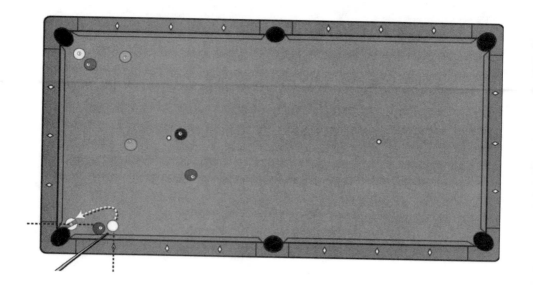

THE VERY EXTREME MASSE SHOT (EQUAL DISTANCE)

Here you assume all kicking paths are blocked, and the only way to make this striped ball is to get the cue ball to go out from the side rail towards the middle of the table and then reverse back towards the striped ball. This can be accomplished with an extreme masse shot. The key to this shot is determining where to contact the cue ball with the cue tip. The best way to determine this point is to place your left forearm over the striped ball and the tips of your fingers over the cue ball. Now place your right forearm perpendicular to the rail and the tips of your fingers touching the tips of your fingers on your left hand. You have just formed a ninety degrees angle. The halfway point of this angle (45 degrees in this case) is the line pointing at the correct contact point on the back of the cue ball.

Aim your cue stick along this line to give you a reference point on the back of the cue ball. Now raise the butt of the cue stick until it is perpendicular to the table and aim at this spot on the cue ball. You will have to reverse your back hand grip. Next, make a fist with your bridge hand as you will need to shoot this shot freehand. The cue stick will go through the junction of your first finger and thumb, but the rest of the fingers will form a fist. Lightly drop the cue stick straight down through the cue ball and into the cloth, and the cue ball will "squirt" out a little to the right. Then the back spin will stop the cue ball's forward momentum and propel the cue ball back towards the striped ball.

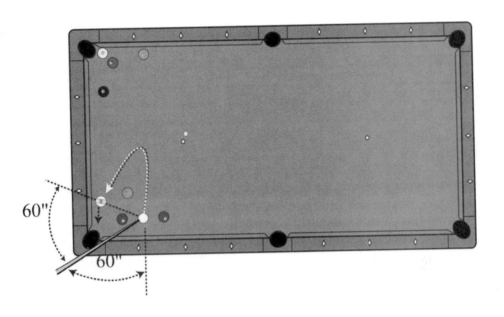

THE VERY EXTREME MASSE SHOT (UNEQUAL DISTANCE)

This shot is very similar to the previous shot except the cue ball and object ball are not equal distances from the side rail cushion. But the calculation of the contact point on the cue ball is the same. Again form the angle with your forearms and fingers just as before (dotted lines). This time that angle is 120 degrees. Now divide the angle in half (60 degrees) and place your cue stick along this line. Your cue stick is now pointing at the back of the cue ball where it must be contacted by the cue tip. Again, raise your cue stick perpendicular to the cloth and aim at the contact point on the back of the cue ball. Use a forceful loose good follow through stroke. You need to stroke through the cue ball, striking the cloth of the table with the cue tip. This shot will need to be hit a little more forcefully than the previous shot as the cue ball must go out farther towards the middle of the table. As before, the cue ball will squirt out a little to the right before the reverse spin brings it back towards the striped ball.

Both of these extreme masse shots are very difficult and normally reserved for the advanced players. Only practice these shots on your own table with an old cue stick. Also be sure your cue tip is nicely rounded to prevent more damage to the cloth. Do not practice this shot in a billiard establishment without permission from the owner.

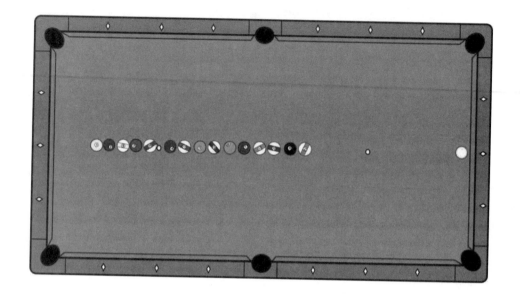

THE BEST MASSE DRILL

If you really want to improve your masse skills, this is the best drill designed to accomplish that goal. Line up all fifteen balls down the center of the table as illustrated. Place the cue ball close to the end rail cushion and also on the centerline of the table. Now before you start, review the mechanics of this shot in the introduction to this chapter. First, try to masse the cue ball towards the right side and hit one of the first five object balls. Now repeat the same exercise on the left side. Once you get a feel for this "area" masse shot, try to hit one of the middle five balls. Again, practice both towards the left and right. And once you get a feel for this area, practice trying to hit one of the last five balls from both sides. This "area" masse shooting will normally be good enough in game situations for the cue ball to contact the intended object ball preventing a ball in hand opportunity for your opponent.

On the other hand, if you want to get even better at this shot, practice this drill aiming at a particular object ball along the line. If you can hone these masse skills to hit the intended object ball consistently, you will have the opportunity to actually "pocket" some of these balls. But remember what I said earlier. Masse shots are extremely difficult shots and extremely hard on the equipment. They are reserved mostly for advanced players.

Chapter Ten
The Jump Shot

This shot, like the masse shot, is tough on the equipment. But again if you are going to play the game on a higher level, the jump shot must be in your arsenal. It is usually used when your masse and kicking routes are blocked. Although some of the really good players are so good with this shot, they use it as their first option. Several years ago, some cue stick manufacturers were making a jump cue called a 747. This was in reference to the large airplane that could take off and fly at high altitudes. This stick was basically a log with a phenolic tip. Even average players could jump the ball with ease using this stick. This stick has since been outlawed and new minimum standards have been established for the jump cue. Like most other shots, there are many components that must be done correctly for the proper execution of a good jump shot. What also makes this shot difficult is that you are shooting from an unnatural position. You will feel very awkward at first when you begin practicing these shots. Below are the various components that are necessary for the jump shot. Understanding these principles will help in the execution of this shot.

THE JUMP CUE

The proper equipment will make learning the jump shot much easier. The legal jump stick today must be at least 40 inches long with a leather type tip no more than 14 millimeters in diameter. They usually weigh less than 11 ounces, are very stiff, and have a very hard leather tip. There are many cue makers making jump cues today, but I believe Ned Morris's Stealth Jump Cue is the best. He has spent years perfecting this legal jump stick. He virtually can jump any ball, anywhere, at anytime. Most jump sticks are two-piece cues like your normal playing stick. Ned's jump stick is a three-piece cue. He has added a small extender to improve accuracy on the longer jump shots. So before you get into the practice shots and illustrations, make sure you have a legal jump cue in your cue case.

THE STANCE

The stance for the jump shot is much more erect than a normal shot. As the butt of the cue rises, the more erect you become. If you are trying to jump a ball close to the rail that is very close to an obstructer ball, you should be standing virtually perpendicular to the floor. Shots off or close to the rail require a more sideways stance. As the cue ball moves towards the center of the table, an even more sideways stance is needed. Also as the butt end of the stick rises, it should move closer to your body. For extreme angles, the butt end of the stick should virtually be next to your cheek or ear.

AIMING

Again, approach the table from behind. Line up as usual as if you are going to shoot the shot. Now slowly raise the butt end of the jump cue stick straight up to the desired position. Your upper body should also move up to a more upright stance. With your head well up over the cue, you are actually shooting this shot with more of your peripheral vision than any other shot. This is why it is imperative that you approach the table perfectly in line with the shot and the butt end of the jump cue brought perfectly straight up. If your initial set up is off line or the cue butt is hoisted sideways, you have no chance of making the shot.

THE CUE BALL

A legal jump shot is one where you actually shoot down on the cue ball, driving it into the cloth and allowing it to rebound at an upward angle.

Shooting underneath or "scooping" the cue ball up is not a legal shot. If you are shooting a ball straight on, the "axis" or line through the center of the cue ball to your tip is parallel to the table. But as the butt end of the cue stick rises, this "axis" line rotates up on the cue ball directly in line with the tip. Just imagine if you held the stick straight up and down over the cue ball. Your new "axis" or center through the cue ball line would now be perpendicular to the table. So even though you may be shooting high up on the cue ball to jump a ball, you are still shooting the cue ball below center or below the "axis" line. Also like the break and masse shot, you should be looking at the cue ball at tip contact.

THE GRIP

There are two types of grips for most jump shots. A general rule of thumb is that when you have to jump a ball greater than 18" away from the cue ball, use your normal loose grip with the full length jump stick. As the butt of the cue rises for shorter jump shots less than

18" or you move more towards the center of the table, the grip should be rotated with your thumb pointing towards the butt end of the cue. On the shorter jump shots, use the shorter (40 inches) two piece jump cue (extender removed) and a loose two finger and thumb grip. The butt end of the cue should virtually slide against your cheek and ear as you stroke.

THE BRIDGE

Form your bridge hand like a normal open bridge. Then rotate your wrist upward, getting the height needed by forming a base with the tips of your fingers. More height can be gained by forming a tripod with your three middle fingers. And even more height can be achieved by using your two longest fingers. Some players with small hands must even form this bridge by balancing it on their longest middle finger. This puts them at a definite disadvantage on this shot.

THE STROKE

This is the final step needed for the proper execution of a jump shot. Now is not the time to become timid. Shoot this like a slower speed break shot with no body movement. Use a very loose grip and a snap action wrist stroke. Be sure to follow through and not hold back on the stick. This stroke is almost like "throwing" the stick at the cue ball. The tip of your cue should contact the cloth and continue for several inches. One of the best "jumpers" I know is Ron Sakahara. He uses a technique of moving slightly side of the cue ball and taking several practice strokes to get the feel of the height and distance needed. Since his initial set up and body position really determine the accuracy of this shot, as he moves back over the cue ball, he is still in perfect line. On the high angle close to the body jump shots, the stroke is almost entirely a snap wrist action with very little forearm movement. The angle of the stick and speed of the stroke will determine the distance and height. The higher the butt of the stick is raised, the higher the release angle of the cue ball from the cloth. The harder the shot is hit, the farther the cue ball will travel before coming back down on the table.

Like the masse shots, these shots are very tough on the equipment. The cloth can be damaged. Balls leaving the table and hitting the floor can be nicked. The rails can be indented with these balls falling from the sky. Furniture can be broken. If you have a table at home, place an old piece of cloth on the bed underneath the cue ball. Or even better yet, glue an old piece of cloth on about a 6" X 6" X 1/4" piece of Plexiglas and use this for your launching area. Do not attempt to practice these shots at a billiard establishment without first obtaining permission from the OWNER.

With all that said, the following illustrations are excellent practice routines to develop a good jump shot. Most of these can be learned fairly quickly. Some will even show how to use english on these shots.

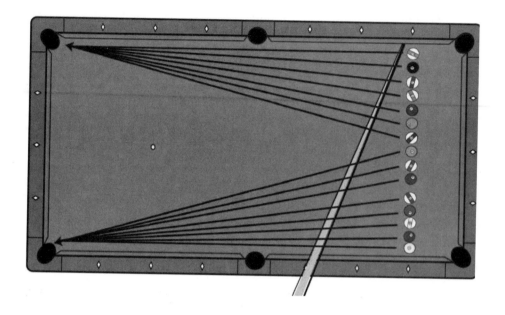

THE BEST JUMP SHOT PRACTICE DRILL

The above illustration shows the best way to practice developing your jump shot. Place all the balls parallel to the end rail at the first side rail diamond mark. Now place an old cue stick with the tip underneath the side rail cushion about 2 inches above the first diamond and extending over diamond #3 across the other side rail. This cue stick barrier will be the lowest closest to the balls and highest the farther away from the balls. Now practice jumping the balls over the cue stick into the corner pockets. Jump the balls closest to the cue stick into the right corner pocket and the balls farthest from the cue stick in the left corner pocket. But before you start practicing this drill, reread the introduction to this chapter. Understanding and executing the proper technique for the jump shot is tantamount to a positive result. Let me again reiterate the key points:

1) Assume a slightly sideways stance.

2) Elevate the butt end of the cue stick to only 30-45 degrees.

3) Aim slightly below the center axis on the cue ball.

4) Use a very loose wrist action forceful stroke.

5) Have a good follow through-throw the stick at the cloth.

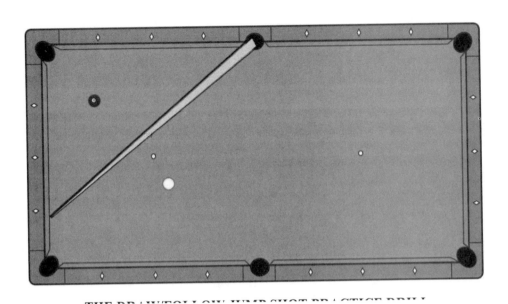

THE DRAW/FOLLOW JUMP SHOT PRACTICE DRILL

Once you have become proficient at jumping the cue ball, the next step is to control the cue ball after it has pocketed the object ball. Place an old cue stick flat on the table between the side pocket and the first diamond on the end rail. Now place the cue ball and an object ball about 10 inches on opposite sides of the cue stick and straight into the corner pocket. First, practice making the object ball into the corner pocket and stopping the cue ball. Now, hit the cue ball slightly below the center axis and the cue ball should draw back up into the cue stick. And finally, strike the cue ball slightly above the cue ball center axis, and the cue ball will follow the object ball into the corner pocket. This is a much more difficult exercise than it looks. If you are having trouble with this drill, go back and practice some more on the JUMP SHOT PRACTICE DRILL. Then come back to this drill and see if your execution improves.

Perfecting the jump shot requires lots of practice. Unfortunately, because it is rough on the equipment, practice time is usually limited. But if you have a good stroke and a complete understanding of the mechanics of the jump shot, you will begin to shoot and execute this shot like any other shot.

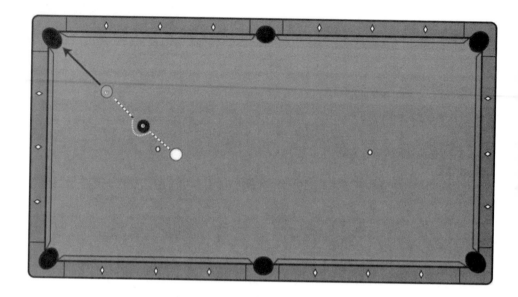

THE SHORT JUMP SHOT

The above illustration shows a more "game like" situation. Most of the time the path to the intended object ball is only partially blocked by an obstructer ball. Practice making the object ball into the corner pocket. Since you only need to clear the side of the obstructer ball, you will only need to raise the butt of the cue about 25-30 degrees and hit slightly below center on the cue ball. Also this is a short shot so you will not need a great amount of force on your stroke. And these partially blocked jump shots are usually shot with your normal playing cue stick.

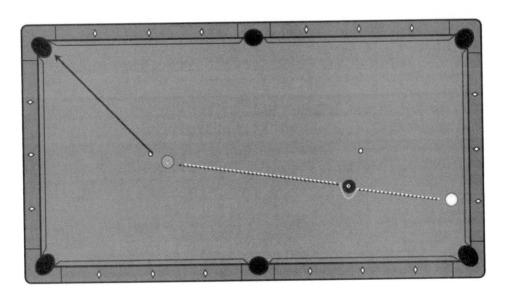

THE LONG JUMP SHOT

These are the types of shots that come up quite often in game situations because your opponent has played a good safety leaving you completely blocked and a long distance to the intended object ball. These shots require the cue ball to go "airborne" a great distance to clear the obstructer ball and contact the intended object ball. Because of this, these are the type of shots where the cue ball leaves the table quite often. The butt of the cue will need to be raised higher on these shots and a more forceful stroke will be needed to keep the cue ball in the air for several feet before it goes over the obstructer ball. The cue ball must come down on the cloth as close as possible to the obstructer ball so the bouncing will be reduced before it contacts the intended object ball. If the cue ball strikes the object ball as it is coming down from the bounce, the object ball has a good chance of leaving the table.

If the cue ball strikes the object ball as it is coming up from the bounce, the cue ball has a good chance of leaving the table. This is why the cue ball must be rolling or bouncing as little as possible when it contacts the object ball.

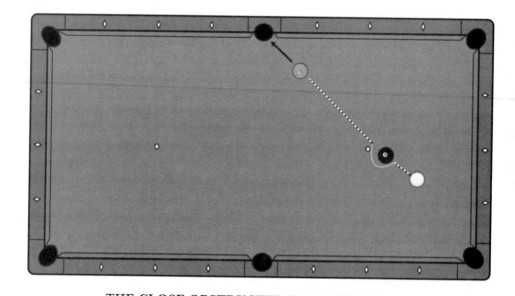

THE CLOSE ORSTRUCTER BALL HIMD SHOT

THE CLOSE OBSTRUCTER BALL JUMP SHOT

When the cue ball is very close to the obstructer ball, the cue ball must almost go straight up in the air to clear this ball. As mentioned in the introduction to this chapter, the technique on this shot is slightly different. First, you remove the extender from the three piece jump cue to give you the minimal legal length size jump stick. Now move your body as close and upright to the shot as possible. Reverse your back hand grip and use only your first two fingers and thumb. Your stroke should be right along your cheek line and as close as possible to your chest. Take a few practice strokes to the side of the cue ball. Use a forceful but very loose snap action wrist stroke. The cue ball will be propelled almost straight up in the air over the obstructer ball towards the intended object ball.

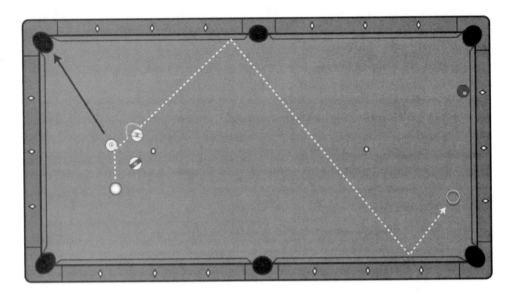

THE JUMPED OBJECT BALL POSITION SHOT

When you normally think of a jump shot, the normal jump shot is to have the cue ball jump an obstructer ball and contact the intended object ball. In the above eight ball game scenario, you have a direct shot on your solid ball but you cannot get the cue ball to the other end of the table for your next shot because your opponents striped balls are blocking the cue ball path. Your goal here is to pocket the solid ball into the corner pocket and have the cue ball jump the obstructer ball. The cue ball would then continue into the side rail cushion and rebound across the table for position on the next solid ball at the other end of the table.

Shoot the shot like a normal jump shot using the full length jump cue or even your own playing stick. Do not elevate the butt end of the stick too much as you only need the cue ball to slightly leave the cloth bed. This shot can be executed two ways. First is to have the cue ball come down on the cloth slightly before the object ball. The rebounding cue ball from the bed cloth will strike the object ball above its horizontal centerline axis, causing the cue ball to go airborne over the striped obstructer ball.

The second way is to have the cue ball actually come down on top of the object ball and carom over the obstructer ball. Sometimes this way causes the object ball to leave the table. The key to this shot is not to have too much angle on the object ball. The shot is very difficult and gets harder as the angle to the object ball increases.

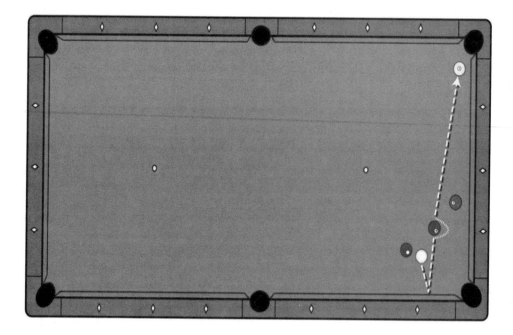

THE CUSHION FIRST JUMP SHOT

Every once in a while, you will be faced with virtually no way to hit the intended object ball. The above diagram illustrates one of those examples. Obstructer balls are blocking all of the kicking, masse, and normal jumping routes. But if you remember the discussion earlier regarding the cue ball or object ball leaving the table when the collision of the two balls is not parallel to the surface of the table, you can use that same principle to your advantage on this shot.

Instead of trying to jump over the obstructer ball too close to the cue ball straight on, you can actually aim into the cushion away from the obstructer ball as if you were going to kick the intended object ball into the corner pocket. Now raise the butt end of the cue stick up and shoot the cue ball into the cushion. Use a snap action loose wrist moderate stroke. The goal is to have the cue ball leave the cloth and come down again slightly before the cushion. As the cue ball bounces up from the cloth and into the cushion, it will become airborne and go over the top of the obstructer ball towards the intended object ball in front of the corner pocket.

This is really a "touch" jump shot. If the cue ball is hit too softly, it will not clear the obstructer ball. If it is hit too hard, it will go completely off the table. These cushion first shots are very difficult to learn. You will find that the initial practicing of these shots will cause the cue ball to leave the table quite often. These are last resort shots and the more prudent shot is to take a deliberate foul and try to tie up several balls to make it more difficult for your opponent to run out.

Chapter Eleven
Position Play

This is how the professionals make this game look so easy. They understand and are able to execute all the concepts previously discussed in this book. By knowing the tangent line, english, and cushion angle behavior, they are able to move the cue ball around the table with uncanny accuracy. All shots become easy when they are less than 3 feet long with a 20-30 degree angle. Understanding virtually all the previous chapters is a must for the discussions and illustrations in this chapter.

The key to playing position is to always be on the right side of the object ball and to stay away from straight in shots (remember rule #6 from the 10 WINNING RULES FOR 9 BALL). When you are on the right side of the object ball, the rebound angle of the cue ball off the object ball usually is the normal angle to proceed to your next shot. When you are on the wrong side of the object ball, this usually means your cue ball must be forced to travel away from the tangent rebound line. This results in the cue ball traveling greater distances and/or multiple rails to reach the desired position for the next ball. When a player is playing well and positioning "whitey" exactly where he wants it on each shot, it is called "connecting-the-dots." Or another way to think of this is if the player were able to have the cue ball in hand after each shot, he would place it on the table at the same spot the cue ball landed after he actually shot each shot. The following 3 things must be mastered for proper position play:

SPEED

After the object ball is pocketed, the cue ball must then roll to a designated spot for the next shot. Without proper knowledge of the speed needed, it will either roll too long or too short. Improper execution here will get you quickly out of line. You usually think of speed control as the finesse part of the game. Before you get down on the shot, the speed needs to be determined. Then your warm up strokes should reflect the same rhythm to obtain the desired speed. For slower finesse speed shots, move your bridge hand slightly more forward and shorten the stroke by not bringing it all the way back to your knuckle. The slower the speed needed, the shorter the stroke. For fast speed or power shots, DO NOT increase the normal stroke rhythm. This will not give you more speed and destroys accuracy. This aspect of the game can only be learned with lots of practice. The following outside factors that can affect speed are:

1) Humidity - Think of the cloth like a golf green. It also picks up moisture when it rains outside greatly reducing the roll.

2) Cleanliness of the balls and/or cloth - Dirt causes friction inhibiting ball roll.

3) Newness of cloth-New cloth is extremely clean and tight. Watch the balls actually slide here especially after leaving the rail.

THE TANGENT LINE

The rebound angle of the cue ball off the pocketed object ball must be known for each shot. This angle is the direction the cue ball will travel after contact with the object ball. If you have a hard time referencing this angle, try lining up the object ball to the pocket with the tip of your cue stick on the cloth underneath the ball. Now imagine a line from the cue ball to this point. The angle that these two lines form will be the same angle the cue ball will be released from the object ball on contact. Some players like to stand behind the pocket the object ball is to be pocketed in and visualize both the angle needed to pocket the ball and the tangent line rebound angle the cue ball will travel.

ENGLISH

Many times, the normal rebound angle of the cue ball is not the desired path you want the cue ball to travel. This is when spin or english on the cue ball is needed to alter the direction the cue ball will travel. You may need to shorten this angle with follow (high english) or widen the angle with draw (low english). Or you may want to change the rebound angle of the cue ball off the cushion by adding side (left or right) english. Or you can even do combinations of these (high right, low left, high left, & low right). There are literally hundreds of contact points on the cue ball to give you various english combinations from moderate to extreme. Also remember the more english you apply to the cue ball, the more those three bad words that effect accuracy begin to enter into the picture-throw, deflection and squirt (Chapter 13).

It takes years of practice to master the position play aspect of the game. Getting the cue ball to end up at an exact spot requires the proper speed, angle, and english on each and every shot. And by the way, don't forget to pocket the object ball. That is always your #1 priority. Understand and practice the following illustrations. They will give you the basic foundation upon which to build your position play skills.

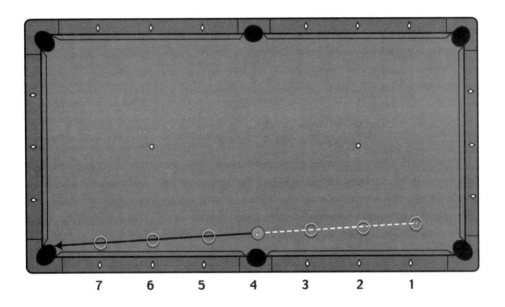

7   6   5   4   3   2   1

FINESSE SPEED SHOTS

When you only need to move the cue ball a short distance, move your bridge hand closer to the cue ball to about 50% of your normal bridge length. Also move your back hand slightly forward to keep your forearm perpendicular to the cue stick. You should think of about 3 different finesse speeds. With finesse speed #3, on the back stroke bring the cue tip all the way back to the fulcrum (junction of the stick and your finger) of the bridge. Finesse speed #3 will move the cue ball the farthest. With finesse speed #2, bring the cue stick back only about half the distance from the cue ball to the fulcrum of the bridge hand. And with finesse speed #1, only bring the cue stick back about one quarter of the distance. As you can imagine, this speed will move the cue ball the least. Your warm up strokes should be slower than normal and very deliberate. Be careful not to bring the cue stick back any farther than the finesse speed you have determined. Use your normal follow through on all three speeds.

Practice the above illustration. Your goal is to pocket the object ball into the corner pocket and follow the cue ball along the same path. With a finesse speed #1 shot, the cue ball should travel to diamond #5. With a finesse speed #2 shot, the cue ball will travel to diamond #6. And with a finesse speed #3 shot, the cue ball should travel to diamond #7. Once you become proficient at this exercise, then practice drawing the cue ball back to diamonds #3, #2, & #1. Control of the draw shot is always more difficult.

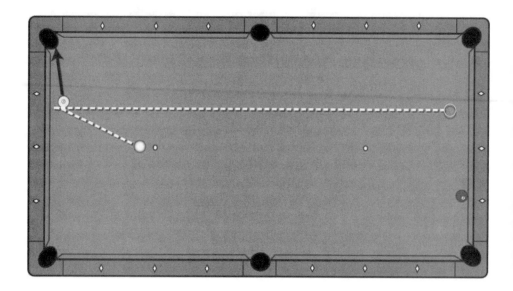

THE STRAIGHT UP THE RAIL POSITION

Over the years, I have seen the above illustration shot incorrectly countless times. Here you need to pocket the object ball close to the end rail cushion into the corner pocket and have the cue ball go to the other end of the table for position on the next shot. I have seen players scratch into the side pocket(s) and corner pocket(s) many times. I have seen the cue ball hit the protruded corner of the side pocket cushion and rebound back to where it came from. The correct way to shoot this shot is just to bring the cue ball straight up the table. This way no pockets or rail cushions can get in the way. With an understanding of the tangent line, you know the cue ball will head straight into the end rail cushion after pocketing the object ball. If the cue ball is hit dead center and has no spin, the cue ball will rebound off the end rail cushion straight up the table to the other end. Now all you have to control is the speed. And since this next object ball can be made easily from about the second diamond in, that gives you about a 4 foot landing area (two feet to the cushion and two feet rebounding from the cushion).

Practice this position shot as it is a key position shot in nine ball since the cue ball is constantly traveling long distances up and down the table. Keep the object ball close to the end rail cushion between the first and second diamonds but vary the cue ball placement.

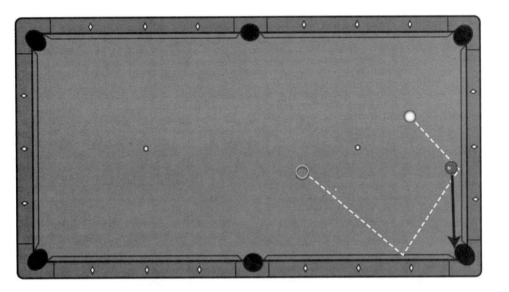

THE TWO RAIL CENTER TABLE POSITION SHOT

Most good players know they can make most shots when their cue ball is in the middle of the table, their bridge hand is stable on the bed cloth, and the table does not infringe upon their proper body position. Being able to position the cue ball to this spot is an advantage in virtually all pocket billiard games. Practice the above illustrated shot. Place the object ball close to the end rail cushion between the first and second diamond and the cue ball at about the junction of the first diamond on the end rail and the first diamond on the side rail. Use a soft to moderate stroke with right english only. The cue ball will spin off the end rail cushion to the side rail cushion and rebound to the middle of the table.

Much of the velocity of the cue ball comes from the spin as it rebounds off the cushions. Place a small round target (about 8 inches in diameter) in the middle of the table and practice landing the cue ball within the target. Once you become fairly proficient at this position shot, try "cheating" the object ball to one side of the pocket or the other and use varying amounts of side spin to obtain the same center table result. This is another key position shot in all pocket billiard games.

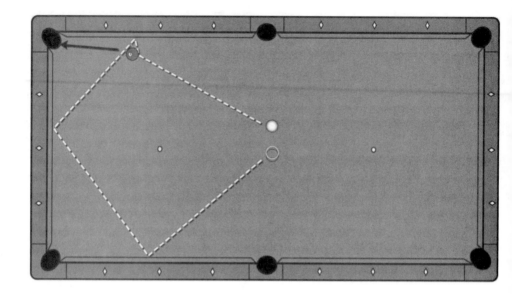

THE THREE RAIL CENTER TABLE POSITION SHOT

This three rail position shot is very similar to the two rail position shot. This time the object ball is close to the side rail cushion just below the second diamond, and the cue ball is in the center of the table. Again the goal is to pocket the object ball and move the cue ball back to the center of the table. Do not underestimate how important these shots are. Time and time again, both the previous shot and this shot come up. Having the confidence in both of these shots that you can pocket the object ball and get the cue ball back to the center of the table can improve your game dramatically.

Again, let me repeat what I said regarding the last shot. Good players can make most shots from the center of the table. Use only left english and a more moderate stroke than the previous shot as the cue ball must rebound off one more cushion and travel a little farther. Trying to draw the cue ball back to the center of the table too often results in a missed shot or a scratch into the side pocket.

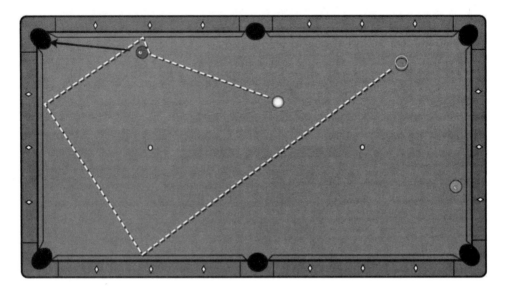

THE THREE RAIL END TABLE POSITION SHOT

This shot is only an extension of the previous shot. Set the shot up exactly like the previous illustration. This time a more moderate stroke will be needed to move the cue ball three cushions to the other end of the table. Again use left english or a little high left to give the cue ball more forward roll. Do not use much high english as it will widen the rebound angle and possibly cause a scratch into the corner pocket at the other end of the table.

As a rule of thumb, always go forward with the cue ball when the object ball is close to the side rail cushion and below the second side rail diamond and the cue ball is close to the center of the table. Trying to draw the cue ball backwards usually causes a scratch into the side pocket. Some of the better players are able to draw the cue ball with extreme english or a slight masse shot. I do not recommend this for average players as this can destroy the accuracy of the hit on the object ball. Have you ever heard a player say, "I missed the shot but I have perfect shape on my next ball." Don't fall into the same trap unless you are playing me!

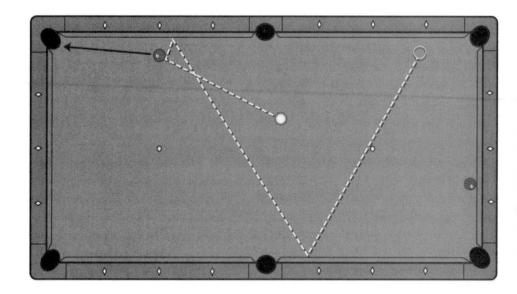

THE TWO RAIL DRAW END TABLE POSITION SHOT

This illustration is a variation of the previous page.   Set the shot up as before, but this time place the object ball close to the side rail cushion and slightly above the side rail second diamond. Since the cue ball is in the middle of the table, the rule of thumb says you are able to draw the cue ball back missing the side pocket. By applying low right (mostly right) english on the cue ball, the cue ball will rebound off the side rail cushion towards the other side rail cushion up from the side pocket. It will then rebound off this cushion for position on the next ball.

Because you are reversing the direction of the cue ball, these shots require a more moderate stroke. But do not hit the cue ball too hard as this can reduce the rebound angle and possibly cause a scratch. Accuracy is important on this shot, so be sure to use a smooth loose moderate good follow through stroke.

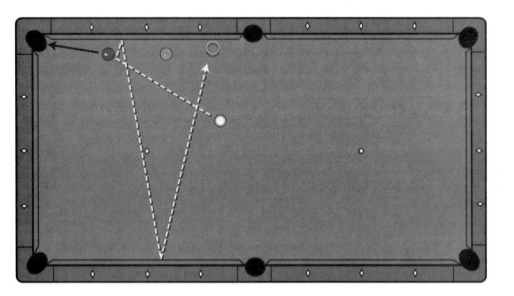

THE TWO RAIL CUT POSITION SHOT

This is another shot that comes up quite often in nine ball and is also a good one pocket shot. The goal here is to cut the object ball closest to the pocket along the side rail cushion into the corner pocket and get position on the object ball behind it. In one of the previous examples, you know you can make the shot and position the cue ball three rails towards the same side of the table as the next object ball. But this will leave a fairly long shot on the next object ball. Or you could cut the object ball in with a dead center cue ball hit and have the cue ball rebound straight across the table and back for a shot on the next object ball into the other end corner pocket. But this would leave a long shot and possibly a difficult cut shot if the cue ball were not positioned properly.

Most players prefer to cut the object ball into the corner pocket with a little (1/2 tip) low english. This will cause the cue ball to rebound off the side rail cushion across to the other side rail cushion and rebound back to about side rail diamond #3 above the next object ball. The key to this shot is not to use too much draw english. Too much low english will invariably cause the cue ball to scratch into one of the side pockets. The other key is to use the proper speed on the cue ball. Coming up short on this shot can leave a very difficult cut shot.

Practice this shot and all of the previous shots discussed so far in this Chapter. If you are a nine ball player, one or more of these position shots are used on virtually every rack. Being able to pocket the object ball and control the cue ball on these shots can vastly improve your game.

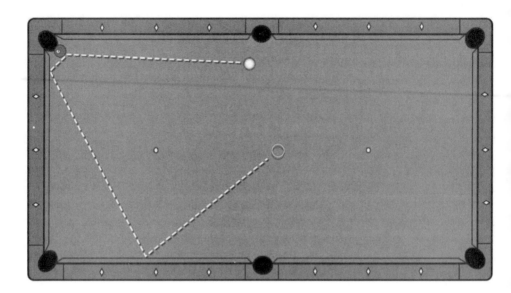

THE "JAWS" OBJECT BALL CENTER TABLE POSITION SHOT

This is another shot that is misplayed too often. Many times the player will attempt to come off the end rail cushion straight to the middle of the table with the cue ball. Too often this results in a scratch into the side pocket or the cue ball running long towards the other end of the table. The proper way is to shoot this shot with left english, spinning the cue ball off the end rail cushion to about the second diamond on the side rail cushion. It will then rebound off this cushion towards the center of the table. This takes away the possibility of a side pocket scratch. Second, the cue ball rebound path of the side rail cushion is now on a direct path towards the center of the table. Now the only thing that needs to be controlled is the speed of the cue ball.

Shoot this shot with about a half ball hit on the object ball and about 1 tip of left english. The half ball hit on the object ball can be accomplished by aiming the tip of the cue stick at the edge of the object ball. Use a soft stroke because of the velocity of the cue ball will come from the side spin as it rebounds from the cushions. Shooting this shot too hard can result in a scratch into the corner pocket.

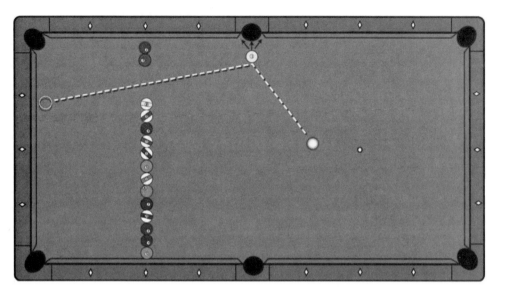

THE SIDE POCKET BLOCKER DRILL

This drill has many names (football, linebacker, blocker, etc.), but it is the best drill for developing your side pocket position skills. Because the object ball is close to the side pocket and the side pocket is quite large, the object ball can be contacted by the cue ball at various points and still be made into the pocket. These various contact collision points between the two balls can change the rebound angle (tangent line) of the cue ball. By adding english (especially low) to the cue ball, the rebound angle can be altered further.

Set the above illustration up with the cue ball in the center of the table about 1 diamond up from the side pocket. Place an object ball about 2 inches in front of the side pocket. Use the white donuts for a consistent set up. Now place a series of balls (about 19 for a 9 foot table) in a straight line going across the table at the diamond #2 location leaving about a 2 1/2 ball gap between the last ball and the side rail cushion. Your goal is to make the object ball and have the cue ball proceed down to as close to the end rail cushion as possible without striking any of the "blocker" balls. Also watch out for the scratch. Now move one of the balls from the blocker line to the side rail cushion. The gap is still 2 1/2 balls, but it has moved a little more away from the side rail cushion. Continue moving a ball and practicing this drill until the gap is at the far side rail cushion. You will notice that the farther the gap moves towards the far side rail, the fuller the hit on the object ball is needed and the more low english on the cue ball must be applied.

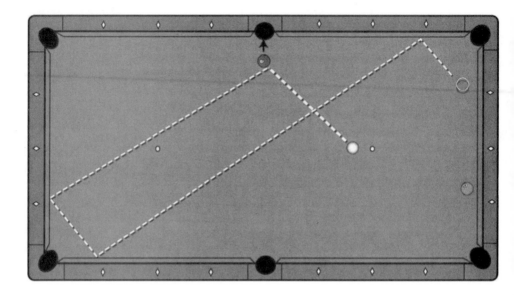

THE 3 RAIL SPIN DRAW POSITION SHOT

Now that you have practiced the previous "blocker" drill, you should have a good feel of how to control the cue ball on these side pocket shots. The above illustration is an extension of that drill. Here you have actually positioned your cue ball incorrectly above the side pocket. You must pocket the object ball into the side pocket and get position on the next object ball at the far end rail. Many players prefer to shoot this shot with low english and a fuller hit on the object ball. This will draw the cue ball to about the first diamond on the end rail. The left spin on the cue ball (picked up from the collision with the object ball) will cause the cue ball to follow the illustrated path towards the other end of the table. Use a moderate speed hit on the cue ball and a loose smooth follow through stroke. This trajectory line to the next object ball gives you about a four foot stopping area for the cue ball where this object ball can easily be made.

There are two negatives to this shot. If the object ball is struck too full and the cue ball has too much low english, the cue ball can actually be drawn into the corner pocket. Conversely, if the object ball is struck too thin by the cue ball and it does not have enough low english, the cue ball will contact the end rail cushion at about the middle diamond and go three rails into the upper right corner pocket. The two keys to this shot are to be sure the cue ball contacts the end rail cushion at about the first diamond (not the pocket or the middle diamond) and to control the speed of the cue ball.

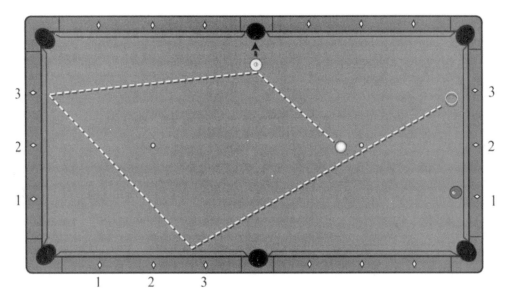

THE TWO RAIL SIDE POCKET POSITION SHOT

This is another way to shoot the previous illustration. This time, the object ball is not struck quite as fully by the cue ball and very little draw english is applied to the cue ball. But you will need to apply about 1 & 1/2 tips of left english to the cue ball. Use a fairly forceful hit on the cue ball, and it will carom off the object ball towards the end rail cushion at about diamond #3. The cue ball will then spin towards the side rail diamond #3 and spin off the cushion towards the opposite end rail at about end rail diamond #3. The key to this shot is to be sure you get enough side spin on the cue ball.

Like the previous illustration, there are several negatives to this shot. If the object ball is struck too thin, the cue ball can scratch into the corner pocket. If not enough left english is applied to the cue ball, it can scratch into the side pocket as it rebounds off the end rail cushion. Also if too much low english is applied to the cue ball, it will contact the end rail cushion at about diamond #2, causing a possible two rail scratch into the corner pocket. The key to this shot is to be sure the 3-3-3 line is followed by the cue ball, and the speed control is correct.

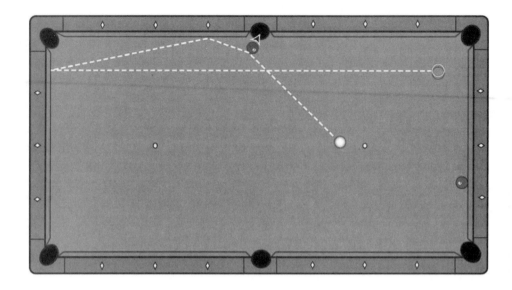

THE OBJECT BALL BELOW THE SIDE POCKET POSITION

Any time the object ball is below the side pocket or very close to the side pocket, the above illustration is the best route to take to get the cue ball back to the far end of the table. Trying to "stun" the cue ball to the end rail and back results in too many cue ball scratches into the corner pocket. Trying to draw and spin the cue ball to the end rail results too many times with the cue ball contacting the first end rail cushion at about the middle diamond. You know from the previous illustrations that the cue ball rebounding from this diamond can cause a scratch into the side or corner pocket. So the best way to shoot this shot is a thin hit on the object ball and right (reverse or hold) english on the cue ball. The cue ball will rebound off the side rail cushion to the end rail cushion and the reverse english will cause the cue ball to rebound off the cushion straight up the table.

There are two keys to this shot. First Is a thin hit on the object ball. Since the object ball is so close to the pocket, pocketing this ball is almost a given. Also too full of a hit can cause a scratch in the corner pocket. Second, the proper amount of right english must be applied to the cue ball. Too much right english will actually cause the cue ball to head towards the corner pocket. Use a moderate to firm stroke because the two cushions and the reverse english will reduce the cue ball velocity.

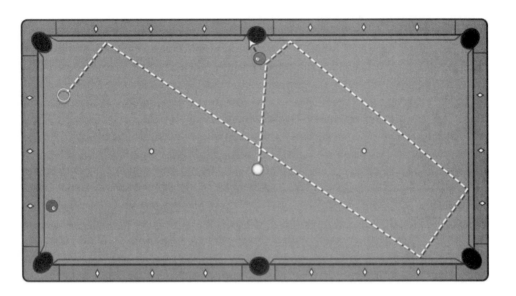

THE ALMOST STRAIGHT INTO THE SIDE POCKET POSITION SHOT

The above illustration is shot incorrectly most of the time by many players (including some good ones). The goal is to shoot the object ball into the side pocket and get position on the next object ball at the far end of the table. Unfortunately, the cue ball has ended up on the wrong side of the object ball in front of the side pocket. Many players will hit the object ball fairly full with lots of right english on the cue ball. This invariably will have the cue ball find the 2-2-2 line (Chapter 4) that will cause the cue ball to go three rails for a scratch into the corner pocket. Or if the object ball is struck too full, the cue ball can go 2 rails and scratch in the side pocket. The correct way to shoot this shot is to cheat the object ball towards the side of the pocket with about a 1/3 ball hit. Use only a dead center ball hit on the cue ball. The collision with the object ball will impart spin (running english) on the cue ball. The cue ball will then go three rails towards the first diamond up from the far corner pocket. This virtually eliminates the possibility of a scratch unless the object ball is struck too thin. Try shooting this shot using a striped ball as the cue ball. Notice the spin the "striped cue ball" picks up from the collision with the object ball even though you are using a dead center ball hit.

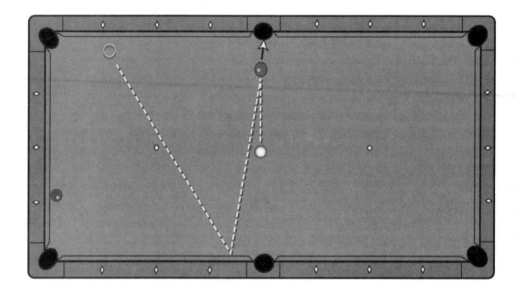

THE STRAIGHT INTO THE SIDE POCKET DRAW POSITION SHOT

Here again you have violated one of the nine ball rules (Rule #6) and gotten straight in position on the object ball with the next object ball frozen on the far end rail. By "cheating" the object ball towards the right side of the side pocket (remember they are almost 2 1/2 balls wide), a small angle is created for the rebounding cue ball. If low right english is applied to the cue ball, the cue ball will draw back to about 1/2 diamond down from the side pocket and spin (right english) off the cushion for position on the object ball frozen on the end rail. I know some of you are thinking to use low left english on the cue ball. Many players have a hard time visualizing the side spin needed on the cue ball when it is coming towards (draw) them rather than away (follow) from them. If you are one of those players, always go to the other side of the table and visualize the necessary spin needed on the cue ball when it contacts the intended cushion. Or another way is to think of what side spin would be needed if you were to follow the cue ball to the opposite rail and just use the opposite side english for the draw shot. Use a firm loose snap action wrist stroke.

Another way to shoot this shot (not illustrated) is to simply strike the object ball slightly off center with a dead center or slightly below dead center cue ball hit. Use a very forceful loose stroke, and the cue ball will "stun" or drift straight down the table towards the end rail cushion.

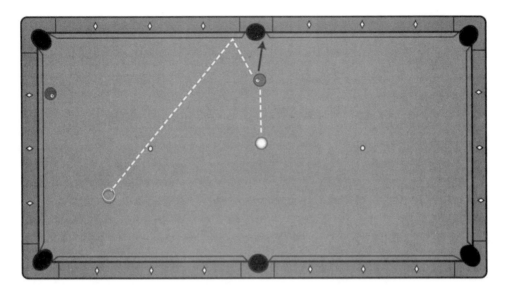

THE STUN /FOLLOW SIDE POCKET POSITION SHOT

The above illustration is a duplicate of the previous diagram except your next object ball is frozen on the end rail cushion towards the other side of the table. Again, you cheat the pocket a little to the right. This will give you a slight rebound angle for the cue ball. By applying high english on the cue ball, the cue ball will go forward to about 1/2 diamond down from the side pocket. Because of the off to the side collision with the object ball, the cue ball will again pick up some side spin. It will then rebound off the cushion and spin towards the opposite side rail. Use a fairly firm loose stroke as this is more of a stun shot rather than a follow shot. If you want the cue ball to head towards the end rail cushion, add a little left english to the cue ball along with the follow. But be careful here as the cue ball can many times find the corner pocket.

Chapter 13 discusses deflection and squirt. After you have read and studied this chapter and its principles, come back and practice these two illustrations using the "off line" stroking method. Many players feel this "off line" shooting method works especially well on these straight in shots. See if it works for you.

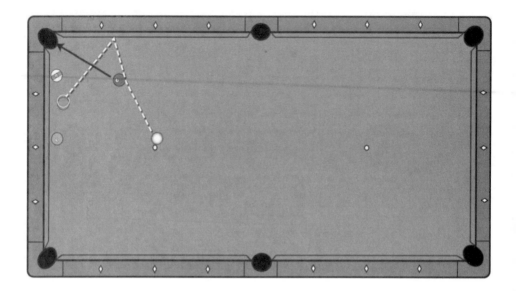

THE INSIDE "KILL" POSITION SHOT

The inside kill position shot is one of the more delicate pool shots. It requires a soft stroke and more of a push type shot. Here again you have ended up on the wrong side of the object ball to get to your next solid ball. Your opponent's striped ball is blocking the upper corner pocket leaving only the bottom corner pocket open for your next shot. If you shoot the object ball with a soft center ball hit, the cue ball will end up in the middle of the table leaving no shot or a very difficult bank on the next solid object ball.

Another way to shoot this shot is to use a very firm stroke on the cue ball with low right english. The cue ball will go three rails around the table towards the end rail cushion where the next object ball is located. Unfortunately, running the cue ball this far (especially when there are other balls on the table) is not a good option. Also there is a possible scratch in both corner pockets. The proper way to shoot this shot is to elevate the butt end of the cue about 6-8 inches. Apply extreme low left english to the cue ball. Shorten your bridge and use a soft extra follow through stroke. You need very little energy to pocket the object ball, but we will need a lot of spin on the cue ball to have it rebound off the side rail cushion towards the end rail.

This shot requires very little practice. Once you understand the proper technique, it becomes only an execution issue.

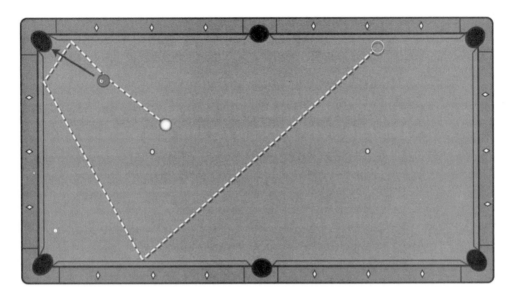

THE THREE RAIL FORCE FOLLOW POSITION SHOT

Under normal circumstances you could easily pocket the object ball and draw back for position on the next object ball at the far end of the table. But assume there are some obstructer balls preventing this path. Assume you only have a forward path to the next ball. You can get the cue ball to the same position spot for the next object ball by using a force follow shot. These are difficult shots because a harder than normal stroke is needed to propel the cue ball multiple rails after colliding with the object ball. A harder than normal stroke always erodes the accuracy of the shot. Use the white donuts and set the above shot up as illustrated. The object ball is aimed just outside the corner pocket. Apply high left english to the cue ball and the cue ball after pocketing the object ball will travel three cushions towards the other end of the table.

The key to this shot is to use a very loose forceful stroke with an exaggerated follow through. It is almost like "throwing" the cue stick at the cue ball but with more control. Try not to put too much left english on the cue ball as this will cause more "squirt" (Chapter 13) further eroding the accuracy of the pocketing the ball. This shot is really a test of how well your stroke has developed. If you are having trouble with this shot, further practice on the stroke builders will be needed.

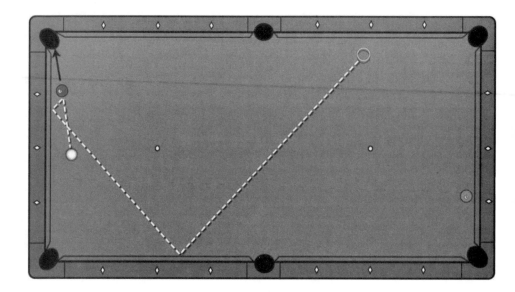

THE POWER DRAW POSITION SHOT

The above illustration shows another "out of position" shot. The cue ball is aimed at the object ball almost straight in to the corner pocket along the end rail cushion, and the next shot is at the other end of the table. One way to get the cue ball up to the other end of the table is with the power draw shot. But in order to accomplish this position shot, several things must be executed perfectly. First, the object ball must not contact the end rail cushion. Because this shot is hit very forcefully, any contact of the object ball on the end rail cushion first will cause the object ball to "rattle" out of the pocket.

Always aim for the center of the opening of the pocket so the object ball enters the pocket cleanly. Second, about 1 & 1/2 tips of low english (be sure your cue tip is well chalked) will be needed to get maximum back spin on the cue ball. And third, a very loose back hand grip and a snap action wrist stroke must be used.

Because the object ball is hit very hard by the cue ball and slightly off center, the cue ball will "stun" off the object ball towards the end rail cushion. Then the back spin will take over, causing the cue ball to spin towards the side rail and rebound towards the opposite end rail. Failure to draw this ball properly is usually caused by holding the butt end of the cue stick too tightly. This is commonly referred to as the "death grip." The stroke must be forceful, but the wrist must be loose. You must have a good stroke to execute this shot properly.

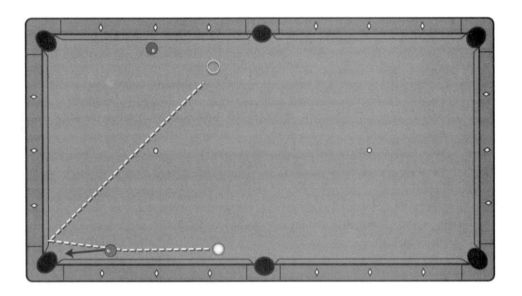

THE STRAIGHT IN POSITION SHOT

Periodically, you will get the dreaded "straight in" position on a shot. This, of course, normally only allows for straight forward or straight backwards movement of the cue ball after contact with the object ball. But it is possible to manufacture a slight angle for the cue ball and still make the object ball. In the above illustration, the cue ball path can be altered by applying high right english. Use a moderate to firm stroke and aim for a more full hit on the object ball than you would think. The right spin on the cue ball will "throw" the cue ball away from the object ball a little towards the right after their collision. Then the high english will drive the cue ball forward towards the end rail cushion about 2-3 inches to the right of the pocket. Now the right spin on the cue ball will cause it to rebound off the end rail cushion towards the other side of the table.

There are two keys to this shot. First, be sure to aim the object directly into the pocket. Even though you are adding right english to the cue ball, the forceful stroke will impart a negligible amount of "throw" on the object ball. The natural tendency is to account for the throw on the object ball from the side spin on the cue ball. This usually rattles the object ball away from the pocket. Second, be sure to use only about 1/4-1/2 tip of right english on the cue ball. This will give enough spin for the cue ball to carom slightly to the right before the follow english takes it to the end rail cushion. Also staying close to the perpendicular center of the cue ball keeps cue ball squirt to a minimum, ensuring better accuracy on the shot.

189

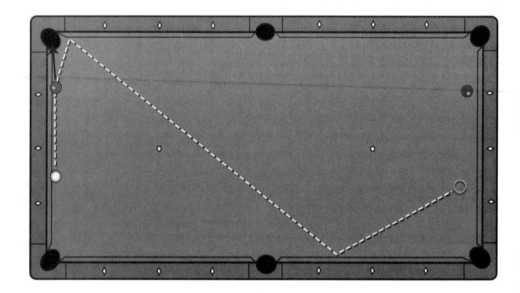

THE ADVANCED STRAIGHT IN POSITION SHOT

The above illustration shows one of the most difficult position shots in pool. You have violated two of the nine ball rules (rules #6 & #9). First you have the dreaded straight in shot. Second, you have left the cue ball very close to the cushion. Both of these problems make it extremely hard to get the cue ball to the other end of the table for the next shot. But it can be accomplished by using a combination jump and masse shot. First, raise the butt end of the cue stick about 6-8 inches. Second, apply high right english to the cue ball. And third, use a moderate to forceful stroke. You will need to aim slightly to the right of center on the object ball as the cue ball will "squirt" towards the left due to the off center hit on the cue ball and the downward stroke. The object ball must then be contacted first by the cue ball, allowing the cue ball to move into the end rail cushion after contact with the object ball. The high right english on the cue ball will spin the cue ball towards the side rail, and it will then spin off the side rail cushion towards the other end of the table.

There are several key factors for proper execution of this shot. First, if too much of a downward hit or too much force is used on the cue ball, either the cue ball or object ball or both can leave the table. Second, a very loose back hand grip is needed with an exaggerated follow through on the stroke. This is another one of those shots where you are almost throwing the cue stick at the cue ball. If you are making the object ball but following the cue ball into the pocket, the cue ball is probably contacting the cushion first.

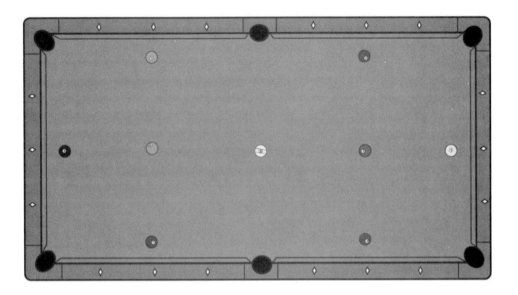

THE BEST NINE BALL POSITION PLAY DRILL

This practice position drill will do more to improve your run out game than any other drill in this book. Spending an hour a day on this drill for one month will improve your game dramatically. Guaranteed! This practice drill virtually incorporates everything previously learned in this book. If you are having a problem on a particular shot, go back to the chapter that discusses that shot and determine what you forgot or what you need to do to execute the shot properly.

Set the 1 through 9 object balls on the table as illustrated. At the beginning, place the lower numbered balls at one end of the table and the higher numbered balls at the other end of the table. Place the nine ball in the center of the table. Also place the object balls that are close to the rail about 2-3 inches away from the cushion. Your goal is to take ball-in-hand on the one ball and try and run out the table. If you are a very good player, randomly place the 9 object balls around the table and try to run out the table. And if you are an excellent player, move the balls that are close to the rail closer to the cushion (0-1 inch) and try to run the table. The key to all three run out scenarios is to always play three balls ahead and always stay on the right side (not the wrong side) of the object ball with the cue ball. This will allow for the proper angle and the least amount of movement of the cue ball as it travels to its proper position for each of the next object balls.

191

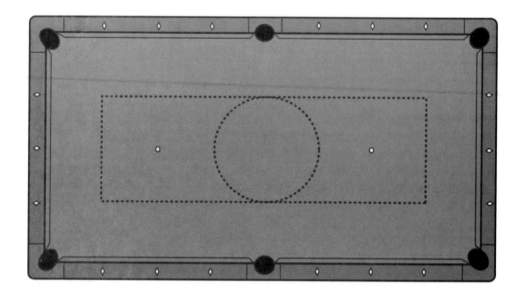

THE OPTIMUM POSITION ZONE

The last two diagrams in this chapter will do more for your position game than anything else. They require no practice whatsoever. You only have to memorize the diagrams. The above diagram shows the optimum cue ball placement for almost all shots. Keeping the cue ball within the dotted lines ensures the following:

1) Gives you an area for a stable closed bridge hand on the cloth bed.

2) Gives you a level cue stick because bridging off the rail always elevates the butt end of the stick.

3) Gives you proper body alignment and position because the table does not hinder your proper body position and other tables/chairs in the room are not in the way of your stance when shooting off the rail.

4) Keeps you from using the bridge or cue extender.

5) Gives you a good rebound angle off the cushion for the cue ball to get position on the next object ball most of the time.

If you watch the professional players play nine ball, they invariably bring the cue ball back into this middle circle after each shot. They can virtually make almost any shot and get their desired cue ball position from this area. Try it yourself. Arbitrarily place an object ball on the table. Now place the cue ball anywhere within the circle. I bet you can make the ball. So when in doubt, always play for position within the dotted circle.

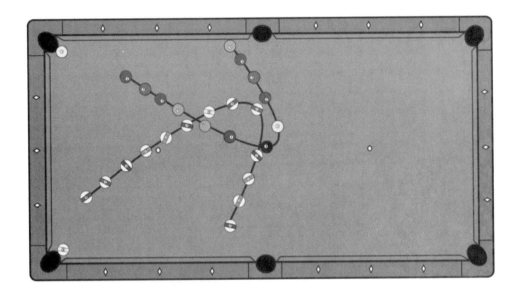

THE "DEAD" ZONE

I bet most of you will have no idea what the above diagram represents. It represents the closest the cue ball can get to the corner object ball without compromising your body position against the table or needing a bridge or cue extender to reach the shot. The next time you go to the pool table, do the following two exercises. 99.9% of all pool players have never done this exercise.

Place a striped ball in front of the bottom corner pocket as illustrated. Now with the cue stick in your hands, place your bridge hand on the cloth bed close to the end rail cushion as close to the striped ball as possible without compromising your body position. Place an object ball in front of your cue tip. Now move up the table about 6 inches and repeat the exercise. Continue moving all the way around the table placing more balls on the cloth. Anything within this "striped ball thumb print" area will not be able to be reached without a mechanical helper or compromising your body position. Never shoot a shot with the cue stick "underneath" your body or your back hand touching the bumper. You have entered the "dead zone".

Now duplicate the exercise with a solid ball in front of the upper corner pocket. This time start close to the side rail and as far past the side pocket that you can reach. Continue moving around the table placing a ball every six inches. This should form a slightly smaller "solid ball thumb print" dead zone area. The two areas are not the same as they were done for a six foot right handed player. Memorize your own particular "dead zones".

Chapter Twelve
Specialty Shots

The following illustrated specialty shots are not trick shots but shots that come up periodically in game situations. It is more important to understand how to execute these shots than to spend a lot of time practicing them. If you can understand the reasoning on these shots, the execution is usually fairly simple. Learn them all. You will probably amaze some of your pool playing friends when you execute one of these shots. Or maybe they will just think you are "lucky." I always like it when my opponent thinks I am "just lucky."

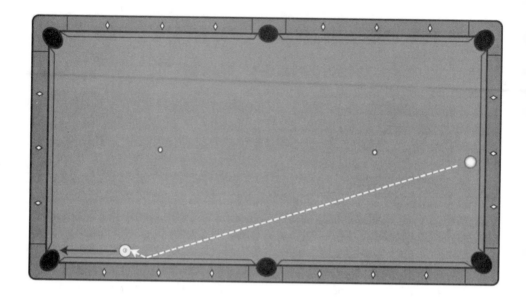

THE RAIL FIRST LONG SHOT

Many players (even good ones) shoot the above shot incorrectly. Here the object ball is close to the cushion (less than 1/2 inch) and close to the pocket (less than 2 diamonds away). The cue ball is at the other end of the table close to or even frozen to the end rail cushion. This is a very difficult shot. Most players will try to shoot the object ball directly into the corner pocket. About 90% of the time, this shot is missed because the object ball is hit too full, causing it to hit the side rail cushion first. The natural tendency is to almost always drive the object ball into the side rail cushion. The right way to execute this shot is to have the cue ball contact the side rail cushion first just before it contacts the object ball. This rebound angle off the cushion first of the cue ball towards the object ball will actually cause the pocket to play a little larger than the straight shooting line from the cue ball to the object ball. In fact, the object ball is almost always made by contacting the right inside part of the pocket and avoiding the side rail cushion altogether.

If the object ball is missed towards the end rail, the cause is because the cushion and ball were contacted at almost the same time. If the object ball hits the side rail cushion, the cause is the cue ball contacting the cushion too far away from the object ball. Practice this shot using a soft center ball or slightly above center ball hit on the cue ball. You will find that this shot is much easier than it originally looked.

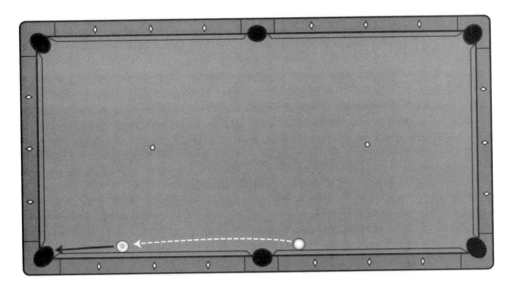

THE BALLS FROZEN TO THE CUSHION SHOT

Here both the object ball and cue ball are frozen to the rail. Again, most players will shoot this shot incorrectly by trying to aim directly at the object ball. Most of the time, the cue ball will be driven into the side rail cushion before it strikes the object ball. The object ball is almost always missed because of the less than full hit, resulting in the object ball also being driven into the side rail cushion.

The proper way to execute this shot is to shoot the cue ball softly, slightly away from the cushion with low left english. The cue ball will first start out going away from the cushion, but the low left spin will bring the cue ball back to the cushion. The left spin will then hold the cue ball on the cushion and into the bed trough as it rolls down the table to the object ball. The trough in the felt is created by the junction of the balls and the cushion. The felt is slightly more worn down along the rail, creating a slight indentation in the bed. Just look at the felt on a table. Notice the lighter lines (from polish & dirt) 1 & 1/8 inches (one half the diameter of the balls) from the cushion all the way around the table. Be sure to shoot this shot softly. If you shoot too hard, the cue ball will not come back to the cushion. Also too firm of a hit can cause the cue ball to follow the object ball into the pocket.

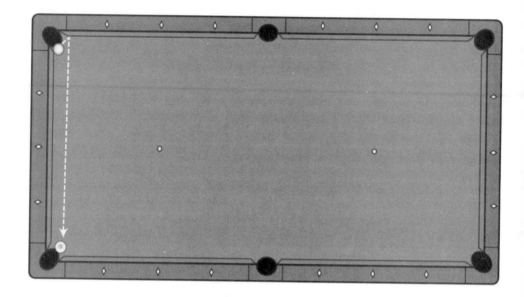

THE CORNER HOOKED KICK

This is another shot that looks more difficult than it is. The object ball is close to the pocket but you let the cue ball roll too far, and it is up against the side of the other corner pocket blocking the path to the object ball. From the kicking chapter, you know several ways to kick at this ball. But assume all those routes are blocked. Another way to shoot this shot is to shoot the cue ball directly into the cushion at the junction of the side of the pocket and the side rail cushion. In other words, right at the protruded cushion junction. The way to aim this shot is to place your thumb directly over the protruded corner. Now place the cue stick over your thumb and the center of the cue ball. This is the shooting line to the corner.

Shoot the shot softly with a level cue stick and high english. The tendency of most players is to shoot too much into the side of the corner pocket, causing the cue ball to contact the end rail cushion. Always aim this shot by aiming a little more to the high side of the protruded junction.   Practice this shot until you get a feel for the proper angle needed. Once you can consistently make the object ball in the "jaws," move the object ball either higher in the pocket or more towards the end rail cushion. Adjust your known angle slightly to make these balls either higher or lower in the pocket.   See, I told you this shot is not as difficult as it looked.

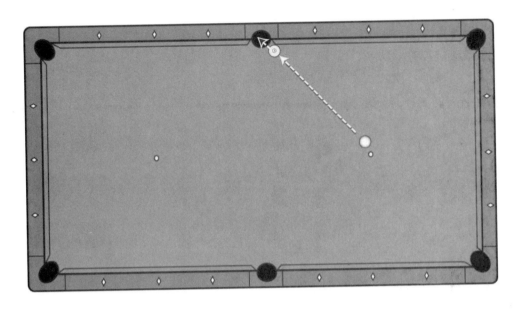

THE FROZEN TO THE CUSHION SIDE POCKET SHOT

This is another one of those shots that looks impossible but can be made quite easily. Here the object ball is very close to the side pocket but it is frozen to the side rail cushion. The cushion is blocking the path into the pocket. But there is a way to actually physically widen the opening of the side pocket. Remember when I discussed the banking principles in Chapter #5; the harder a ball is hit into the cushion the more the cushion will be compressed. That same principle can be applied to this shot. If the object ball is hit straight on with a dead center ball hit on the cue ball and a very forceful stroke, the object ball will first move straight ahead, compressing the corner of the side rail cushion at the opening of the side pocket. This compression (moving the cushion more in towards the rail) of the cushion is in essence widening the opening of the side pocket.

After the object ball has moved forward and compressed the cushion, the side of the cushion can force the object ball to go slightly to the left. But since the side pockets are very wide and by now the object ball has proceeded deep into the pocket, the object ball will continue to the back of the pocket and into the hole.

There are several keys to the execution of this shot. First, more than 1/2 of the object ball must be on the pocket side. Second, the shot must be fairly straight on (all the energy of the cue ball must to transferred to the object ball). And last, a very forceful center cue ball hit is required.

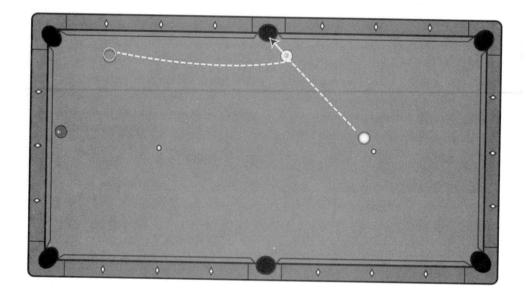

THE SIDE POCKET STUN FOLLOW SHOT

This is another one of those shots that you got yourself into, the dreaded straight in position, and you must move the cue ball to the other end of the table for the next shot.
This can be accomplished with a stun follow shot. By cheating the object ball ever so
slightly towards the right side of the side pocket, a slight tangent rebound angle can be
created for the cue ball off the object ball. If the object ball is struck very forcefully with
a dead center or slightly above center and a solid hit, the cue ball will first bounce a little back and a little to the left. Then the forward momentum will take over, causing
the cue ball to roll towards the end rail for position on the next shot. A very loose forceful stroke is needed to get the proper stun action on the cue ball.

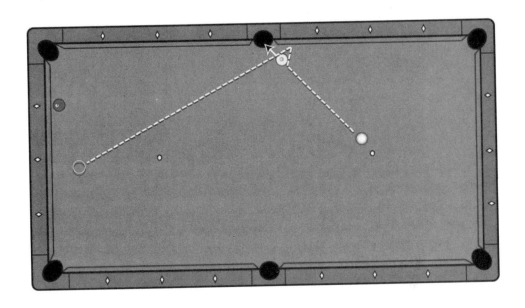

THE EXTREME ENGLISH SIDE POCKET POSITION SHOT

This is another one of those shots in which you ended up on the wrong side of the object ball. Here the object ball is close to the side rail and side pocket, and the cue ball must travel to the other end of the table for the next shot. You could shoot the shot with low right english on the cue ball and bring it three rails towards the other end of the table. The problem with this is that there are several pockets the cue ball could scratch in. Second, you would probably end up on the short side of the object ball and our speed control would have to be perfect.

The proper way to execute this shot is cut the object ball into the side pocket with extreme (about 1 1/2 tips) left english on the cue ball. Aim the object ball wide into the pocket with the thinnest hit possible. This will keep as much spin and energy on the cue ball as possible. The cue ball will carom off the object ball towards the side rail cushion and spin towards the end rail for position on the wide side of the object ball. Use a soft to moderate stroke with a long follow through because the cue ball spin will do most of the work.

Since I mentioned aiming wide into the side pocket, I would like to comment on all angle cut shots into this pocket. On all cut shots into the side pocket, always aim towards the high side. Even if less than 1/2 of the object ball contacts the protruded cushion corner, it has a good chance of going into the pocket. On the other hand, any contact of the object ball with the downside rail cushion first negates any ball pocketing possibility.

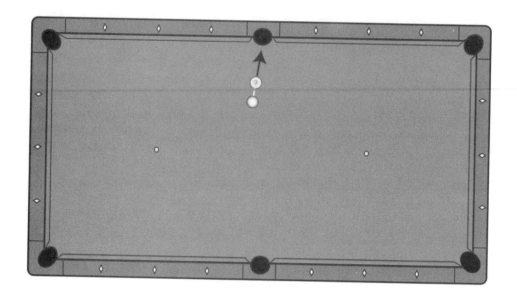

THE TOGETHERNESS SHOTS

The only thing worse than a straight in shot is a straight in shot where the cue ball and object ball are both very close (1/2-2 inches) together. This is a situation where togetherness is not a good thing. The problem here is not in pocketing the object ball but in preventing a double hit causing a foul. There are several ways to approach these shots. The best way is to move your bridge hand as close as possible to the cue ball. I have seen some players actually get the cue ball between their fingers while other players will fold their middle fingers under their palm. Second, after you have positioned the cue stick in your bridge hand, squeeze the cue stick. This will prevent the cue stick from going forward as you slide your back hand forward to your chest. Remember when I talked about the stroke, your chest is what stops the forward movement of the cue stick. Now with the bridge hand very close to the cue ball and the back hand at your chest, the forward stroke is limited to an extremely short distance. Loosen the bridge hand grip on the cue stick and push your back hand into your chest. Hopefully, the object ball will be pocketed without committing a foul.

Another way to shoot this shot is to get the butt end of the cue stick as low as possible and shoot as high as possible on the cue ball. The cue tip will proceed over the top of the cue ball preventing a double hit. And last, this shot can be shot like the safety shot in Chapter #3. Place the cue stick flat on the table with the tip under the edge of the cue ball and pull straight up. Various game situations will determine which approach is best.

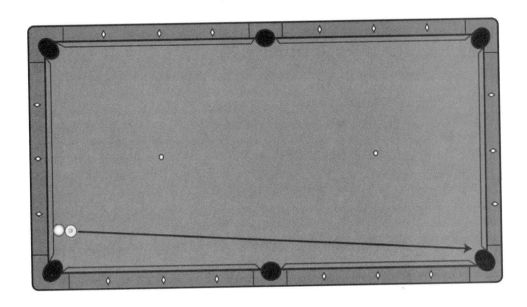

THE CUE BALL FROZEN TO THE CUSHION
AND OBJECT BALL SHOT

When the cue ball is very close to the object ball and there is very little angle, there is always the possibility of a double hit on the cue ball, causing a foul. The above illustration is a perfect example of this concept. Even though the shot is lined up straight into the corner pocket, the closeness of the two balls creates a possible foul situation. But a way to eliminate the possible double collision foul is to aim the cue ball directly into the cushion rather than straight ahead into the object ball. The cue ball will compress the cushion and rebound towards the object ball. Since the shot is already lined up towards the pocket and the two balls are extremely close together, the object ball is easily pocketed into the corner pocket.

There are several keys for the proper execution of this shot. First, the cue ball must be contacted as high as possible with a fairly level cue stick. Second, use a very loose back hand grip and a moderate stroke. The loose back hand grip and the high hit on the cue ball will cause the cue tip to bounce off the cue ball and continue over the top of the cue ball preventing a cue ball foul. And last, be sure to contact the cue ball along its perpendicular center axis. Any side spin applied to the cue ball can "throw" the object ball off its intended path. This shot also only needs to be hit as hard is if you were going to shoot it straight into the pocket. The tendency of most players is to shoot this shot too hard. Use a nice smooth loose moderate stroke.

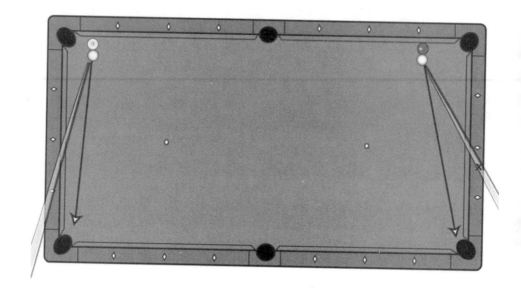

THE CUE BALL FROZEN TO THE CUSHION
AND OBJECT BALL BANK SHOT

This shot is very similar to the previous shot except this time the object ball is frozen to the cushion and the touching balls are lined up straight across the table and not towards a pocket. By shooting at a slight angle into the object ball, the object ball can be compressed into the cushion and banked back into the corner pocket. Again, use a very high center axis hit on the cue ball but use a much more forceful stroke. On the illustrated shot on the left, the frozen balls are at about the 1/2 diamond mark along the side rail cushion. Aim the cue stick at the cue ball with the butt end of the stick over the first diamond on the end rail. Use a moderate to forceful loose snap action wrist stroke, and the object ball will be banked back into the corner pocket. The shot on the right has the frozen balls at about the first diamond mark along the side rail cushion. This time, line the shot up with the butt end of the cue stick over the 1 & 1/2 diamond mark on the end rail. Again, use the same loose stroke and the object ball will be banked back into the corner pocket.

One negative on the shot is that the cue ball can cling to the side rail cushion as it goes up the table and can scratch into the corner pocket. I usually will not attempt this shot unless there are other obstructer balls blocking this scratch path of the cue ball. Also a one diamond bank is about the maximum that will work on these frozen cushion bank shots.

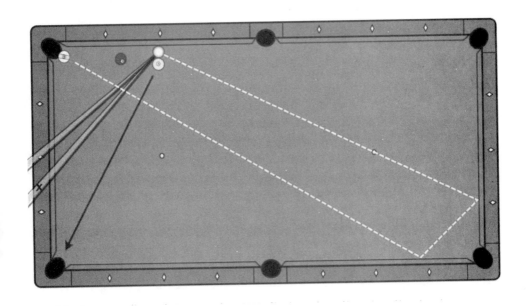

THE BALLS FROZEN TO THE CUSHION CUT/KICK SHOT

Here the cue ball is frozen to the side rail cushion at one end at about the second diamond up from the side pocket and an object ball at the other end. The two frozen balls are aimed straight across the table at the opposite rail second diamond. There are actually two shots involved here. If the intended ball to be pocketed is the frozen object ball, aim into the cushion with the butt end of the cue stick over the 1 & 1/2 diamond mark on the end rail. The cue ball will compress the cushion and rebound back into the object ball cutting it into the corner pocket. Again, aim high on the cue ball with a moderate stroke and a very loose back hand grip. The cue tip must glance off and over the cue ball to prevent a cue ball foul. A tight or "death" grip on the cue stick will prevent the cue tip from bouncing away from the cue ball.

The second shot is a kick shot at the ball in front of the corner pocket. Here the direct path to this object ball is blocked by an obstructer ball and the frozen object ball prevents almost all kicking paths. This time, you aim at the cue ball with the butt end of the cue stick over the middle diamond on the end rail. This slight change in the angle from the first shot will cause the cue ball to compress the cushion and completely miss the frozen object ball. The cue ball will continue towards the end of the table rebounding two rails back towards the object ball in front of the corner pocket. Notice how this angle is different from the normal kicking path discussed in Chapter #4. The extreme high hit on the cue ball and the english picked up from the frozen rail cushion will alter the normal kicking path.

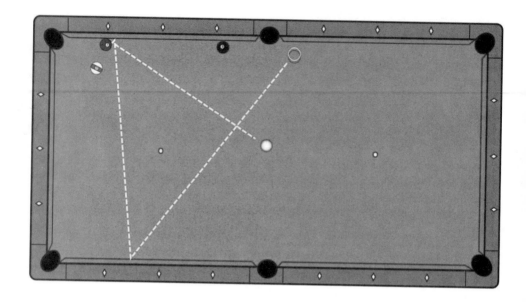

THE DRAW ENGLISH SPIN POSITION SHOT

Imagine you are playing eight ball and your last solid ball and the eight ball are both frozen to the side rail cushion with the cue ball in the middle of the table. Pocketing the last solid ball by slow rolling the cue ball will leave a very difficult long cut shot past the side pocket on the eight ball. This shot is normally missed, resulting in a sell out to your opponent as his last striped ball is close to the pocket. The normal path to the eight ball is to go three rails with the cue ball and get above the side pocket for a shot into the corner pocket. Unfortunately, this path is blocked by your opponent's striped ball.

Chapter 11 shows the easiest way to shoot this shot, but this is another way. Shoot this shot applying low left english to the cue ball. The cue ball will draw over to the opposite side cushion, and the left spin will cause the cue ball to rebound towards the other side of the table about one diamond up from the side pocket. This will leave a much easier shot on the eight ball into the corner pocket.

This is a very difficult shot normally reserved for advanced players. The key to this shot is to actually have the cue ball contact and compress the side rail cushion first. It will then spin into the object ball, pocketing the object ball into the corner pocket. The cue ball will then carom off and draw slightly backwards towards the opposite side rail cushion. This slight manufactured angle works synergistically with the cue ball side spin to better position the cue ball above the side pocket on the opposite side rail.

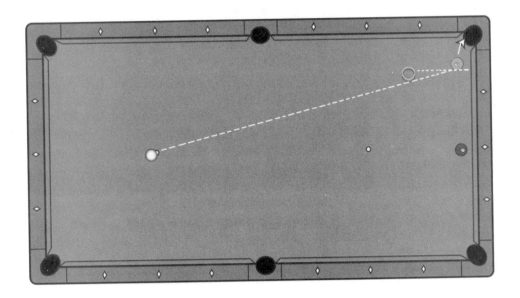

THE DRAW DRAG SHOT

Here you must cut the object ball into the corner pocket and hold the cue ball close to the end rail for position on the next shot. But the cue ball is at the other end of the table. One way to shoot this shot is to just slow roll the cue ball. In other words, just stroke the cue ball very softly. There are two problems with this approach. First, any time you alter your normal stroke, accuracy is compromised. Second, any unevenness of table bed or any dirt (small pieces of chalk) can greatly alter the path of the slow moving cue ball.

Most of the good players prefer to shoot this shot with a "draw drag" stroke. Use a normal stroke and about 1 - 1 & 1/2 tips of low english applied to the cue ball. This low english will impart reverse spin on the cue ball as it proceeds down the table. This reverse spin will cause increased friction (drag) on the cloth, slowing the cue ball as it approaches the object ball. As the cue ball gets closer to the object ball, most of its forward momentum will be reduced, and the cue ball will begin to roll forward. This slow rolling cue ball will pocket the object ball and rebound off the cushion only slightly for position on the next object ball. The most important aspect of this shot is to be sure the cue ball is struck very low along its centerline perpendicular axis. Any side spin (along with the low english) applied to the cue ball can alter the cue ball path. Try experimenting with this shot, using low left and low right english. Watch how the cue ball path is altered both before and after contact with the object ball.

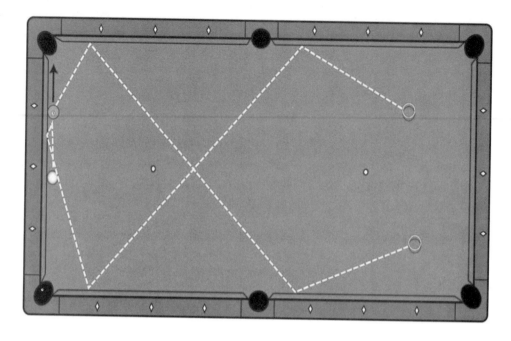

THE FROZEN TO THE CUSHION DRAW/FOLLOW SHOT

The above illustration shows one of the most difficult shots in pool. It can only be executed if you have developed an excellent stroke. An inferior stoke will not allow you to get the action on the cue ball needed to get it to the other end of the table. If you are unable to execute this shot, I suggest you go back to the stroke builders and refine the mechanics of your stroke. Here both the cue ball and object ball are frozen to the end rail cushion, and you must get to the other end of the table for the next shot.

There are two ways to move the cue ball up the table depending on which side of the table you need to position the cue ball for the next shot. The first way is to use extreme low left english on the cue ball. The cue ball will draw back off the end rail cushion and rebound towards the side rail. It will then spin off this cushion towards the other end of the table as illustrated. You will need to aim a little left of center on the object ball as the low left hit on the cue ball will cause it to "squirt" a little to the right. Use a very forceful snap action loose wrist stroke. The second way is to apply high right english on the cue ball. The cue ball will rebound off the end rail cushion and follow towards the side rail. It will then spin off this cushion towards the other end of the table.

On this shot, you will need to aim only slightly right of center on the object ball as the high right hit will cause the cue ball to "squirt" left only a little. On tight pocket tables, I suggest you forego this shot as the margin for error for pocketing the object ball is just too small. Play the percentages!

Chapter Thirteen
Deflection, Squirt, Cling, Throw and Skid

These problem areas are the science part of the game. All of these can effect the accuracy of the shot. It is important to understand each of these principles because they will effect your aiming point on many shots. Many very good players do not understand the "why" part of these principles, but through countless hours of repetitive play, their brain has learned the "how" part and is able to naturally adjust the aiming point. Once you understand these principles, you will learn with practice how much you will need to alter your aiming point with your stroke and cue stick on various shots.

DEFLECTION

When the cue ball is firmly hit dead center down the table, the cue stick continues past where the cue ball was in a straight line. Now if the cue ball is hit off center, the tip of the cue is now contacting the cue ball at an angle because the cue ball is a round sphere rather than a flat surface. Upon contact, the cue tip will "deflect" into the cue ball. The shaft will actually bend slightly, and the cue ball will travel off the intended path. This difference in the actual traveled path versus the intended path is caused by the inherent "deflection" in the cue stick. All cue sticks have deflection characteristics. Some have more than others. Listed below are some of the things that effect these characteristics:

1) **Diameter of the shaft.**
2) **Stiffness of the shaft.**
3) **Taper of the shaft.**
4) **Type of wood used in the cue stick.**
5) **Type of ferrule.**
6) **Hardness of the cue tip.**

Most of the good cue manufacturers today work very hard keeping this characteristic to a minimum. One manufacturer called Predator makes a special shaft called a "314." This shaft is made of concentrically laminated pieces of wood glued together with a foam core down the middle. This shaft is supposed to give the least amount of deflection. This is why all good players have their own cue sticks. They know the deflection in their cue stick and how much to compensate on a given shot.

SQUIRT

Squirt is the result of the deflection of the cue tip off the side of the cue ball. The cue ball will then "squirt" to the opposite side of which it was contacted by the cue tip. The amount the cue ball moves (squirts) away from the intended path is influenced by some of the following factors:

1) Inherent deflection in the cue stick.

2) Speed or force the cue ball is contacted.

3) Distance the cue ball travels.

4) Amount of side english applied.

5) Elevation of the butt of cue stick (masse).

6) Outside factors — ball/cloth cleanliness, humidity, etc.

This principle can be demonstrated very easily. Take an 8 1/2 X 11 inch sheet of paper and place it on the cloth bed of the table. Place your index finger behind and centered to the paper. Slowly push the paper forward, and it will proceed in a fairly straight line. Do it again with your finger about 1/3 to either side. Notice how the paper begins to move sideways as it moves forward. Move your finger almost to the end. The paper basically tries to just spin on its axis and barely moves forward. Now try this again, using more speed. See what happens?

This is why the professionals use as little side english as possible. Very seldom will they go more than 1 tip away from the center of the cue ball, especially when long distances and extra force is involved. They can get all the action they need on the cue ball with just a little side english, a little angle, and a pure stroke. By developing an excellent stroke and staying close to the center of the cue ball, you can almost eliminate cue ball squirt from your game. But with that said, some good players and even some professionals use a slightly different aiming system on these side english shots. This system is known by various names - Back Hand English, Tuck & Curl, Off Line, Sway, etc.

This system seems to compensate for the deflection and squirt. What you do here is line up the object ball to be pocketed with a dead center ball hit. Take your normal warm up strokes. Once you are SET, move the cue tip to the cue ball by "swaying" your body either left or right depending on the english desired. This keeps the cue stick in line with your body. Also be sure not to move your bridge hand. Now bring the cue stick back and PAUSE. Finally, stroke through and across the cue ball. This system seems to allow for more action on the cue ball with less side english. It can be used anywhere, but seems to work best on maximum squirt and deflection (long and hard) shots. The key to this system appears to be the fulcrum distance from the bridge to the cue ball. The cue stick being moved sideways by the back hand will influence the sideways movement of the tip. Experiment with moving the back hand sideways 6 inches with a 4 inch bridge. Now move it the same 6 inches with a 10 inch bridge. Notice how cue tip movement is influenced by this fulcrum principle. Each player's stroke is a little different and each cue stick has its own inherent deflection. The illustrations and examples on the following pages will help you determine the proper distance for your bridge or even whether this system will work for you.

CLING AND THROW

When two balls collide, they will adhere or "cling" to each other for an extremely brief moment in time before they are released from each other along their tangent line angle. The amount of time the balls cling together depends upon the friction generated at the collision. This "cling time" can be influenced by several factors:

1) The collision angle.

2) The cleanliness of the balls.

3) The humidity in the room.

4) The amount of english (spin) on the cue ball.

5) The speed of the shot.

6) The angle of the cue stick.

The lesser the angle the cue ball strikes the object ball, the longer they cling together. This results in the object ball first moving forward (throw) in the same direction of the cue ball before it is released along the tangent line angle. On thin cut shots, less friction is generated, resulting in less throw on the object ball. The professionals have less of a problem with this than the average pool player because their environment is the same for each tournament. They always play in rooms with new clean balls, and the humidity is controlled. Try this experiment. Find a table with freshly polished new balls and play on it for 15-20 minutes. Now go to another table where the balls are older and dirtier. I guarantee you will start missing shots. If you ever watch a trick shot exhibition, you would be amazed at some of the substances applied to the balls these players use to get the desired result. So the more the cling time is reduced, the lesser the object ball will be thrown off its intended path. Note the illustrations on the following pages to further demonstrate this throw principle.

SKID

Skid is a result of cling and throw. Have you ever contacted the object ball with the cue ball at exactly the spot where you were supposed to, but the object ball did not follow its intended path to the pocket. Professional pool player and world trick shot artist, Mike Massey, recently missed a shot in a Las Vegas professional nine ball tournament due to the object ball "skidding" away from the pocket after its collision with the cue ball. Most of the people watching in the gallery could not believe what they had just witnessed. This phenomenon occurs only rarely but can be devastating to a player's ego. The following factors can influence if and when object ball skid can occur:

1) The cleanliness of the balls.

2) A high english hit on the cue ball.

3) A narrow collision angle—less than 40 degrees.

4) A slow to moderate stroke.

5) The cleanliness and type of cloth.

6) The weight and size of the cue ball.

7) The humidity in the room.

Most tournaments begin with fairly clean balls and cloth. Each time the cue ball is contacted by the cue tip, some of the chalk falls on the cloth and some of it is deposited onto various object balls as they come in contact with the cue ball. Now, if the cue ball contacts the object ball at a location where there is residual chalk on both balls, the cling time between the two balls will increase. Now the object ball will not be released from the cue ball until it has moved a little in the same direction it was contacted by the cue ball. The object ball will first "skid" before it begins to roll along its new tangent line rebound path—usually missing the pocket. Some players even chalk their cue tips over the bed cloth depositing more chalk dust and chips on the playing surface. And some players even place the chalk up side down on the rail. So every time your bridge hand touches the rail and then the cloth on the table, you deposit more chalk dust on the playing surface to be picked up by the rolling balls. And as the balls get dirtier, there is more chance for the object ball to skid on narrow angle cut shots.

High english also contributes to object ball skid. The forward spin on the cue ball can transfer a little back spin on the object ball. The back spin on the object ball and the slide can enhance the skid. If you ever watch the professionals play, they hit the vast majority of these narrow angle cut shots with low english and a fairly forceful stroke. They will even add some outside (helping) english to get the cue ball spinning more. The forceful stroke and the spinning cue ball will allow for the quickest separation of the balls and less chance for skid. They want to "shoot" the ball into the pocket rather than just rolling the object ball towards the pocket. They do not want the table conditions to possibly cause a missed shot. With all that said, I do not recommend this technique for the average player. Hitting the cue ball low and to the side will alter the cue ball path eroding accuracy. So just accept those few times when object ball skid affects your pocketing skills. Remember this occurs fairly rarely so don't blame all your misses on this phenomenon.

Skid can occur even more often on the smaller 3 1/2 X 7 foot coin operated bar tables. These tables use a cue ball that is either weighted or larger so the ball return mechanism will only return the cue ball for continuing play. Also at the Las Vegas tournaments, all of the tables are covered with new cloth that is very slick. Both of these conditions can contribute to more object ball skid. Diamond Manufacturing is now making a coin operated bar table that uses an optical scanner to separate the white cue ball from the colored balls. This will allow for a regular cue ball to be used rather than a weighted, magnetized, or oversize cue ball on these tables.

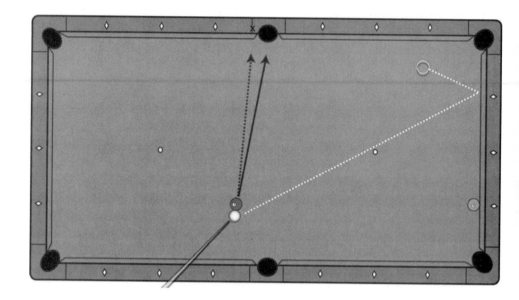

THE SHORT THROW BALL EFFECT

Here the cue ball is frozen to the object ball and the object ball is aimed into the side rail about two inches above the side pocket. By simply aiming at the cue ball, at about a 45 degrees angle as illustrated, the object ball will be "thrown" into the side pocket. Use a soft center ball hit on the cue ball, and the cue ball will stay close to the end of the table for the next shot. Because the balls are frozen together and you are using a soft hit, the two balls will "cling" together for the maximum amount of time. Because of this, the cue ball will force the object ball to first move towards the end of the table. Now after the balls actually separate, the object ball will proceed towards the side of the table but from a different line. This line is a little farther down the table from the original frozen ball line, and the object ball will proceed along this new line into the side pocket. All of this occurs in milliseconds and is not detectable by the naked eye.

Now experiment by hitting this same shot with a firmer stroke. The harder hit will cause less "cling time," and the object ball will only move slightly towards the end rail before moving forward towards the side rail. It will miss the side pocket and hit the side rail cushion between the side pocket and its original aimed line. So the "cling time" between the two frozen balls actually influences the amount the object ball can be "thrown" off its original aimed path.

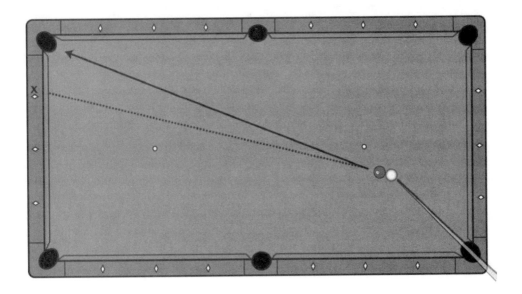

THE LONG THROW BALL EFFECT

The above illustration shows about the maximum amount of "throw" you can get on an object ball with ideal conditions. Here the cue ball is frozen to the object ball, and the object ball is lined up almost at the first diamond on the end rail. And there is a great distance between the object ball and the pocket. Shoot the shot exactly like the previous shot. Aim at about a 45 degrees angle to the lined up shot and use a soft center ball hit. You will only need to shoot this shot hard enough to get the object ball to fall into the corner pocket. This will give you the longest "cling time" and the maximum amount of "throw" on the object ball.

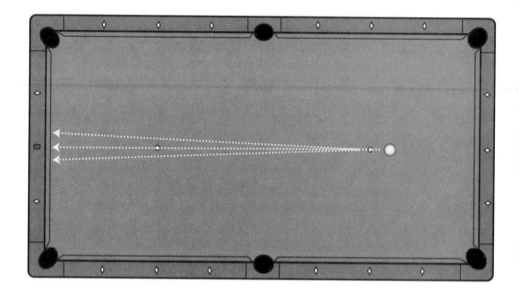

THE CUE STICK DEFLECTION TEST

All cue sticks possess inherent deflection properties. I have heard players say that their cue stick hits true and has no deflection. That is just not true. These players are compensating in their mind and just don't realize they are actually aiming away from the intended contact point on the object ball. Generally speaking, the harder and more outside the cue ball is hit, the more the cue ball will "squirt" away from its intended path.

To test the deflection in your own cue stick, place the cue ball along the long centerline of the table at about the 1 & 1/2 diamond mark on the side rail as illustrated. Now place a cube of chalk over the middle diamond on the far end rail. This piece of chalk will give you a better aiming reference point. Shoot the cue ball with your normal stroke and a dead center ball hit directly at the chalk. The cue ball should contact the end rail cushion directly in front of the chalk. Now shoot the shot again with your normal stroke and one tip of right english. Notice how the cue ball contacts the end rail cushion slightly left of the chalk. Shoot the shot again with maximum (1 & 1/2 tips) of right english. The cue ball will strike the end rail cushion even more to the left of the chalk. Now duplicate both shots with left english. And finally duplicate all four shots with a much harder stroke. Notice how the cue ball is moved even more away from its intended path. Sometimes, another player, standing at the end of the table, can see exactly where the cue ball is contacting the cushion. So on long shots with a moderate to firm stroke, use as little side english as possible.

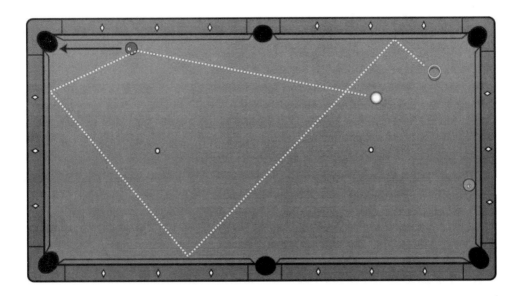

THE REDUCED DEFLECTION THEORY

Here you must pocket the object ball and get the cue ball to go three rails for position on the next object ball. Normally you would line up the shot with high left english to get the cue ball to follow and spin off the cushions for position on the end rail object ball. Because you are using a fairly firm stroke, you know from the previous exercise that the cue ball will squirt a little to the right. We therefore will need to aim a little fuller on the object ball to compensate for the deflection.

Now try the same shot using the aiming method discussed at the beginning of the chapter. Line up the shot with a dead center ball hit on the cue ball allowing for no deflection. Once you have taken your warm up strokes and are SET, move the cue tip to the upper left area of the cue ball by "swaying" your body only. For this left english shot, you would sway your body slightly to the right. If you wanted to apply right english, you would sway your body slightly to the left. Now stroke through and across the face of the cue ball. This "off line" stroke seems to reduce or compensate for the deflection in the cue stick that causes the cue ball to squirt away from its intended path. While this may not completely eliminate the deflection, you will not need to aim as far off the center cue ball contact point on the object ball as you do with just shooting normally with left english. Set this shot up using the donuts for a consistent set up. Now try this aiming and shooting method by varying your bridge length. Try a 4, 6, 8, and 12 inch bridge and see what works best for your particular stroke.

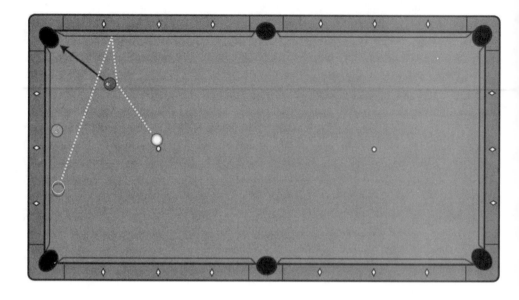

THE REDUCED DEFLECTION PRACTICE SHOT (SHORT)

Now that you understand the principle on this less deflection theory, see if it works for you. Assume you're playing a one pocket game and both object balls must go into the upper left corner pocket. Set the above shot up using the white donut reinforcements for a consistent set up. Go through your normal set up as if you were going to pocket the object ball into the corner pocket with a dead center ball hit. Now move your back hand down and out slightly so the cue tip moves to the upper left of the cue ball. Use a moderate stroke and stroke through the cue ball.

The object ball should be pocketed into the corner pocket, and the cue ball will follow forward spinning towards the side rail cushion and rebound towards the end rail for position on the next ball. If you are missing the object ball, experiment with different bridge lengths. If you are still missing the object ball, adjust your aiming point slightly to allow for some deflection from your cue stick. Practice this shot. Most players are very comfortable using high, low or helping english. But most players are very uncomfortable using inside (opposite or hold) english. This is because this english is not used very much and your brain has not been trained to know exactly where to aim at the object ball. And without the brain being trained, you don't have the confidence on these shots. If you are able to master this theory, you will have much more confidence in these shots and a much higher execution percentage.

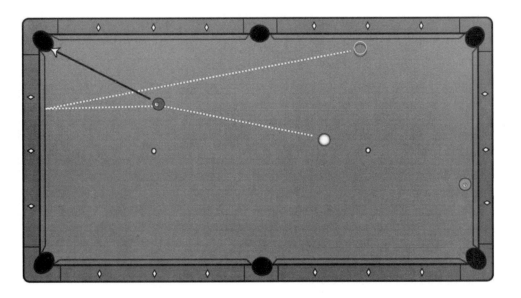

THE REDUCED DEFLECTION PRACTICE SHOT (LONG)

This shot is similar to the previous shot except it is much harder because of the greater distance involved. There is a greater distance between the cue ball and object ball, the object ball and the pocket, and the distance the cue ball must travel for position on the next object ball. The proper way to shoot this shot is just with a little high english on the cue ball, and the cue ball will go two rails for position on the next object ball. But assume there are blocker balls preventing this path. You are limited to "holding" the cue ball on the same side of the table.

Again, set the shot up as illustrated with the donuts. Place the cue ball at the junction of the middle end rail diamond and the diamond #3 on the side rail. Place the object ball at the junction of the side rail diamond #6 and the end rail diamond # 1 & 1/2. Go through your normal set up and aim the shot into the corner pocket with high english only on the cue ball. Now sway your body and move your back hand in towards your body (right handed players). This will now move the cue tip to the upper right quadrant of the cue ball. Use a moderate to forceful stroke and stroke across and through the cue ball. The object ball will be pocketed into the corner pocket, and the cue ball will follow towards the end rail cushion. After contacting the cushion, the right side spin will rebound the cue ball off the cushion and up the table for position on the next shot. The key to this shot is to use a fairly forceful loose follow through stroke. Practice this shot and determine what bridge length works best for you. These are great shots to have in your arsenal.

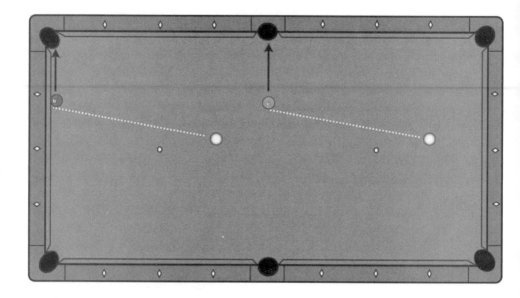

THE FROZEN TO THE CUSHION DEFLECTION CUT SHOT

I feel the illustrated shot on the left is one of the most difficult shots in pool. The object ball is frozen to the end rail cushion and the cue ball is close to the center of the table with about a 70-80 degree angle. But imagine this same shot (distance and angle) was set up for the side pocket as illustrated on the right. This shot looks much easier, but it is really the same shot although the side pocket opening is larger.

There are three ways to shoot these frozen-to-the-cushion large angle shots. First, you can cut the object ball in with a center ball hit on the cue ball just like you would cut the object ball into the side pocket. Other players prefer to cut this ball in with a little "helping" left english. These players would aim slightly away from the object ball as the cue ball will squirt a little to the right. And other players prefer to shoot this shot with right english. Again, you would need to aim slightly fuller on the object ball as the right english will deflect the cue ball to the left of the object ball. If the object ball is slightly off the cushion, I prefer the right english shot. This way if the object ball is missed directly by the cue ball, it may still make the object ball as it rebounds off the rail and spins towards the object ball. Also remember the safety shot discussed in Chapter #3. And always be cognizant of the rebounding cue ball path as these cut shots result in a lot of cue ball scratches.

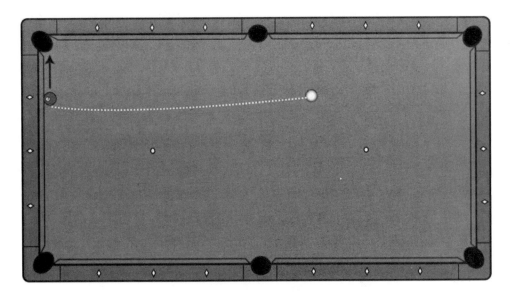

THE IMPOSSIBLE GREATER THAN 90 DEGREES CUT SHOT

Here your opponent has the object ball frozen to the end rail cushion with the cue ball aimed dead on and past the center of the table. He thinks he is going to cut the object ball into the corner pocket. You are probably thinking "No Way" or "Is he crazy?" You may think you have the game won. But if your opponent understands the deflection theories, he can actually manufacture an angle and cut the object ball into the corner pocket. This is done by applying extreme low right english on the cue ball. Aim at about a 1/4 ball hit on the object ball and slow to moderate stroke.

This low right english will cause the cue ball to deflect away from the cue tip and the cue ball will first "squirt" out to the left. So now the cue ball is actually outside of the object ball instead of straight on. As the cue ball proceeds down the table, the low right spin will grip the cloth and bring the cue ball back towards the object ball cutting it into the corner pocket.

This is an extremely difficult cut shot because everything must go perfectly. The cue ball must squirt outside of the object ball. The proper speed must be used. And the proper low right english must be applied to the cue ball to get it to bend back and cut in the object ball. Don't spend a lot of time on this shot, but do understand the deflection theory involved.

Chapter Fourteen
The Ten Winning Rules
for Nine Ball

The most popular pocket billiard game played today in tournaments and leagues is nine ball. It is a fast, exciting, and simple (not easy) game to play. You simply have to make each ball in rotational order (or combination/carom). But the only ball that counts is the nine ball. Whoever makes the nine ball wins. Even luck counts in this game. And some days it seems all the luck and rolls are going in your opponents favor. That is the nature of nine ball. Some days, you run all eight balls but miss the nine ball leaving it in the jaws of the pocket for your opponents. Other days your opponents make the nine ball but scratches, giving you the game. So luck does play an important part in this game. Although it has been said that good players make their own luck and bad players are just more unlucky, I wonder why this is so.

The skills necessary to play this game well are a combination of skills needed for several other games. You need excellent position control of the cue ball similar to straight pool. Good straight pool players can run several racks in a row without ever having a difficult shot. They rely on positioning the cue ball at an exact location on the table after each shot. You need also to play a good strategy game that is very important in eight ball. Good eight ball players will survey the table and decide whether they are going to try and run it out or whether it is better to pocket several balls and play safe, leaving their opponents to kick at their balls. And good nine ball players must possess a good shot making ability similar to the one pocket game. Very seldom are your opponents going to leave you an easy shot in this game to start your turn. So nine ball is a combination of cue ball position, strategy, and shot making ability.

If you have studied, practiced, and now understand the various theories in the preceding 13 chapters, your skill level has greatly improved. This increase in skill level will translate into a higher winning percentage. And if you are a nine ball player, the following ten rules will do more to increase your nine ball winning percentage. Memorize these rules and remember them on every shot. Following these rules alone will increase your nine ball winning percentage.

THE 10 WINNING RULES FOR NINE BALL

RULE #1 When breaking from the side, never allow the cue ball to cross the face of the one ball. This usually causes a lousy break (less transfer of energy) resulting with the cue ball "running" and finding a pocket (usually the side).

RULE #2 Avoid all scratches! If a shot looks like it will result in a possible scratch, it probably will. Don't shoot it!

RULE #3 When playing safe, never leave your opponents with direct shots to a pocket. Force them to bank or play a return safe.

RULE #4 Chalk up before each shot. Or chalk up before each miscue! Most hits on the cue ball in nine ball require a fairly forceful hit with english (hitting away from the center of the cue ball).

RULE #5 Don't stretch. Always shoot with both feet on the floor and use the bridge or cue extender. Never shoot with your cue stick under your body or your back hand touching the bumper.

RULE #6 Always avoid straight in position (unless the goal is only to pocket the object ball). This usually limits cue ball position to only forward, stop, or backward movements.

RULE #7 Always plan for position 3 balls ahead.

RULE #8 Always play the percentages. Know when to hold (shoot) them and know when to fold (safety) them. The smarter players can many times beat the better skilled players.

RULE #9 Keep the cue ball away from the rail. This inhibits a stable bridge and a level cue stick.

RULE #10 Always stay focused, loose and positive.

Below, I have condensed these ten rules into a small area. Print this page, cut these out, and laminate them. Keep this laminated card in your wallet/purse or cue stick case and review it before each match. I guarantee following these rules alone will raise your nine ball winning percentage.

THE WINNING 9 BALL RULES

1) Never let the cue ball cross the face of the one ball on the break.

2) Avoid all scratches.

3) Never leave a direct shot to the pocket when playing safe.

4) Chalk up before each shot.

5) Don't stretch.

6) Avoid straight in position.

7) Play for position 3 balls ahead.

8) Play the percentages.

9) Keep the cue ball away from the rail cushion.

10) Stay focused, loose, & positive.

About the Author

Ron Schneider is an active Certified Instructor by the Billiard Congress of America. He is an instructor graduate of both the CUE-TECH BILLIARD ACADEMY in Carrolton, Texas and the AMERICAN BILLIARD ACADEMY in Garden Grove, California. While his professional and business career as a pharmacist, drug store owner, and chain drug executive and his family have kept him away from pursuing the art of pocket billiards on a more serious level, he has won countless tournaments in various states. This book is the culmination of over 50 years of learning, playing, and teaching the game of pool.